WHICH GOD SHOULD I CHOOSE?

By Ben Kniskern

"Copyright © 2013 by Ben Kniskern

Which God Should I Choose?
by Ben Kniskern

Printed in the United States of America

ISBN 9781625095886

All rights reserved solely by the author. The author guarantees all contents are original and do not infringe upon the legal rights of any other person or work. No part of this book may be reproduced in any form without the permission of the author. The views expressed in this book are not necessarily those of the publisher.

Scripture taken from the New Century Version® Copyright © 2005 by Thomas Nelson, Inc. Used by permission. All rights reserved."

www.xulonpress.com

CONTENTS

Chapter

1. What is Truth?... 9
2. Which God Should I Choose? 17
3. Deadly Cults 21
4. Attractive Articulate 37
5. From Near to Far East, to West, by Southeast Asia 41
6. Far East 51
7. Southeast Asia 55
8. From Moonies to Mormons 69
9. The Oprah Church 81
10. The God of This World 91
11. Another God Worth Mentioning 103
12. Judaism 135

13. Christianity 141

14. Changing God's Recipe 153

15. On the Rocks 171

16. The Change of Life 181

This book is dedicated to my editor, who also just happens to be my daughter and my best friend.

Chapter One

WHAT IS TRUTH?

As you read through this book, you will see that there are a number of gods you could choose to follow. The fact that you are willing to do a little investigative research on the subject beforehand tells me that you may be interested in learning the verifiable truth before you make your decision, and that is commendable. Billions of people have jumped in with both feet, having no prior information at all. Their decision is based simply on their feelings, and by and large they have made the biggest mistake of their lives.

On the other hand, it is possible that you are beginning to read this book, not because you are wondering which god you should choose, but merely because somebody you know is hoping you will make the right choice and cared enough about you to give it to you as a gift. When you see them again, they are likely to ask you if you read it, so — either way — I will try to make it interesting enough for you to hang in there, at least for a couple of chapters.

If you have already made up your mind about which god seems right to you, I will probably not be able to change your way of thinking. I only ask that you view the information I have gathered and pray for direction.

If nothing else, I have summed up my extensive

research and findings in the last couple of chapters, so before you give up, please check those out. I promise you, the information there is life-changing. It is surprising how far we can go through this life and miss out on some of the most amazing things that are available for us to know. If I had not gone searching for them, I may have missed out altogether on much of this information myself.

I'm sure that by now you have heard arguments in favor of many different gods and many different religions. Oddly enough, every religion thinks they are right, but, ultimately, there can only be one truth, and, at the end of it all, only one true God.

The important thing to note is that multiple gods can only coexist in people's imaginations. In reality, there can only be one God, because—by definition—in order to be God, you would have to have absolute authority over all creation. Webster defines God as: "the supreme or ultimate reality; the Being perfect in power, wisdom, and goodness who is worshiped as creator and ruler of the universe."

How could that be shared among many gods? After all, nature proves to us that there has to be a Divine Creator, and so, if the real God created the heavens and the earth, to whom would He be subject; who would He share His title with?

By the way, if you're tempted to question Webster's definition of God, remember this. Nearly every single word you've ever learned the true definition of (and never questioned), was first defined in Webster's dictionary. Coupled with that, any knowledge that you possess of a particular subject, due to your understanding of its interpretation, is based on the definition of the words used to explain it. These definitions also came from this same source. To my knowledge,

What Is Truth?

no educated person has ever seriously questioned the accuracy of Webster's Dictionary.

You've probably noticed, that with all the religions and their gods in the world today, you don't see the many gods themselves fighting—only their followers. This is an important fact to consider when trying to decide which god to follow. You have to remember that there can only be one real God, and that's the one you're looking for. The real God will not be seen fighting with other gods simply because they are not there. They only exist in the minds of the people who make them up or follow them. That being said, of the various gods we mention in this book, only One can be real.

On the other hand, there is always the argument that we are all praying to, or serving, the same god. You hear that a lot, but nothing could be further from the truth. As you read through this book, you will realize that all of the gods mentioned are as different as the people who follow them. They really have little—if anything—in common with the one real God. Anyone who makes this statement (that we all serve and pray to the same god) doesn't have a clue about the variety of details and differences associated with each god or religion.

As I set out to write this book, one of the goals I had in mind was to compare many of today's top religions (by numbers of followers) and the gods they follow. As I began to dig deeper into the more popular religions of today, I realized that many of these religions actually don't have a god at all. They have teachings and practices, leaders, priests and gurus, but no god to follow.

If you are trying to decide which God to choose, religions that have no god are probably not on your list. I will briefly mention the more popular ones so that if they *are* on your list, you can now scratch them off.

Which God Should I Choose?

Remember, our goal is to find the right God—the real One—and do as much as we can in service to Him while we are here in this life. Wasting time chasing after teachings and practices that wind up at a dead end somewhere seriously cuts down on the fairly short amount of time we have here on earth to live a life that has purpose in God's eyes. As we look around, we can see that life is brief, and it would be really good to make the right choice first, or at least sooner than later. Many people (actually billions) make the wrong choice simply because they don't have the opportunity to make an informed decision.

If you knew that an elevator was going to fall ten stories and plunge you to your death, would you get on it? Since there are no warning signs, you probably weren't aware that on average there are 10,200 elevator accidents in the United States each year. In those accidents, an average of 27 people die.

If you knew that Reverend James Warren "Jim" Jones was going to take all your money, property, possessions, and children, brainwash you, move you to a foreign jungle and then make you drink poisoned Flavor Aid, would you have joined his church? Probably not. If you didn't have the factual information ahead of time though, you might have, because there were no warning signs posted.

Before you join any church or religion, just like you are probably going to check out elevators a little more carefully from now on before you get on one, check it out thoroughly—it could be deadly. There are plenty of Jim Jones' in the world today that you need to be informed about so you can make the right choice and choose the right God. There are also many religions and cults in our world today that may not seem all that bad upon first glance, or harmful at all on the surface. And there may be no warning signs posted, but, at the end of the road, there's definitely a huge dead-end sign to go with the skull and crossbones you either missed or ignored.

If you learn what to look for, the false gods and religions are pretty easy to spot. They're getting a little more sophisticated in relationship to mankind's intellect, but the one thing that remains constant is that there can only be one truth.

> All truths are easy to understand once they are discovered; the point is to discover them.
> ~Galileo Galilei (1564-1642)

What is truth, anyway? A lot of times, the answer depends on who you ask. There are a variety of definitions for truth in the dictionary which pretty much all point back to the same thing, but some of the definitions seem a little more complicated than they really need to be. I have simplified it a little and defined truth as "the absence of all lies." That's pretty simple, and not all that arguable. If there is absolutely no lie in it, then it has to be the truth.

A famous soap company used to boast that their soap was 99 44/100% pure. What did that make it? Tainted! One hundred percent pure is pure. Anything less is tainted—not pure at all.

Sherlock Holmes said, "How often have I said to you that when you have eliminated the impossible, whatever remains, however improbable, must be the truth?" (Sir Arthur Conan Doyle)

Since truth is the absolute absence of all lies, and since God absolutely cannot lie, we can conclude that God is the truth. Any god that is involved in a situation where there is even the slightest lie or deception cannot be the real God, because found in the real God is the absence of all lies. Some truth, or partial truth, is not truth at all. Better said, partial truth is a lie with some truth in it.

If I am known as a guy who tells the truth *most* of the time, that still makes me a liar. At that point, how do you know when I'm lying and when I'm telling the truth? You can't. Anyway, you can never be sure. How can you trust someone who is capable of lying? And so, how can you trust a god that is involved with or based on lies? Doesn't that in fact make him or her a lie as well?

This will help anybody who is trying to decide on and choose the right God, because you will find lies—however slight—and deception—however subtle—in every god you examine, until you come to and examine the right one.

WHAT QUALITIES SHOULD YOU BE LOOKING FOR IN THE GOD YOU SEEK?

As deceivers become more cunning and inventive, the one seeking truth must become more knowledgeable. It would be a good idea to contemplate what the characteristics of the real God might look like. You'd be surprised what a simple exercise like that can accomplish. It will really narrow down the list when considering which God you should choose. God has placed in each one of us an emptiness that only He can fill.

It stands to reason therefore, that we should be able to figure out what the real God should be like. If you were to make a list, what would be on it? First, in my mind I guess, is that He would have to be the One who created everything that there is. There couldn't be anything that He didn't create, because where would it have come from? Then, I would think that He should be all-powerful, (in complete control of everything). He should also be all-knowing (having perfect knowledge of all that there is). I would expect as well that He should be ever-present (being everywhere at once). There should be no deceit found in Him. He should be the absolute truth. In addition, I would expect Him to be all-loving. He should be the pure essence of love. The real God would love me and would have created me for a purpose. He would not have me here just by chance. In fact, the real God would have made everything for a purpose, and He would have made it possible for me to find out about Him and have a relationship with Him. He would also be the One who is eternal. The real God would have no beginning and no end.

I would have all of these things on my list as I start comparing the numerous gods out there, seeing how they stack up against these distinctions.

As we go step by step through the many gods that are available to us, it will become pretty apparent that not only do none of these false gods meet *all* of the requirements that would make them God, but plainly, they don't even meet *one* of them. The real God has made it so that no false god can possess even one of His attributes. Once you realize that, finding the right God becomes a much more manageable task.

Chapter Two

WHICH GOD SHOULD I CHOOSE?

Which god should I choose, or which god is right for me, are very good questions. The fact that you are even asking such a question shows that you have come to the place in your life where you are at least pretty sure that there really is a God, and maybe it would be a good idea to find out more about Him. The scary part is that there are many gods to choose from today. Even scarier than that is the fact that many more gods have come and gone throughout human history. This proves that all of the extinct, historical gods (at least) were all false gods made up by human imagination. Sadly, all of the people who followed and served them chose the wrong god and ended up wasting the life that the real God had given them. In actuality, they lived for nothing.

Obviously, the God we choose should not only have the qualities that we seek in a God, but also be real, and able to prove it. He should be able to prove who He says He is, or at least we should be able to determine He is real by the evidence He leaves us. This is not too much to ask, and in fact the real God wants us to seek

Him and find Him. It's pretty hard to find anything, though, without clues, so the real God has left us all kinds of clues to help us find our way to Him, if only we will look. In the end, finding Him is better than finding hidden treasure.

The problem is, I guess, that the world we live in today is like a supercenter for gods. There are as many choices of gods as there are vehicles on a car trader website. And how do we arrive at a choice when shopping for a vehicle? It has to appeal to us, for starters. It has to be the right color, the right size, sometimes economical, sometimes luxurious. It has to meet our needs. It may have to be sporty, or possibly bulky enough to carry many passengers and maybe even a payload. Sometimes, it may be an old vehicle we seek—one that's been around for a long time, and others times, brand new. You may need more than one car. You may need a fleet.

It's like that for many people when they set out to choose a god. That's exactly why there are literally billions of people following a wrong, false god. Some choose their father's god. That would be like buying an Oldsmobile because that's what their father drove, and his father before him. Some choose their god by feeling. They choose the one that gets them the most emotional, like a European sports car. Others choose the most luxurious one, such as a Cadillac. The one that fits their pricey lifestyle, or makes them look the best. The one that makes them appear successful and rich. And then there are those who choose the one that many others have, like an SUV, thinking, in order to have that many followers, it must be the right thing for me, too.

There are plenty of gods to choose from, it is true—but only one can deliver on the promises He makes. So, the real God will be one who keeps His promises.

Think about some of the false gods that we've heard

of. Perhaps the most famous of which (at least in history books) were the Greek gods. Ranging from Aphrodite to Zeus there were countless numbers of those with varying titles like Apollo, the god of music; Ares, the god of war; Athena, the goddess of wisdom; and on and on they go.

The ancient Egyptians had over 2,000 named gods including Ra, the sun god; Isis, the god of magic; and even the Pharaoh himself. In fact, many leaders of many nations throughout history (called an *imperial cult*), like the Caesars of Rome and the Emperors of Japan, have been considered, at least in their own minds, to be gods.

Knowing from history that it is possible for entire nations to worship gods that are nonexistent or narcissistic men or women who believe themselves to be gods, and considering that there are more than 730 established religions in the world today which are broken out into more than 3,200 different sects, it makes the task of choosing the right God (one that transcends time and is truly eternal) a very serious endeavor. Because out of thousands, there can only be just one true God.

If you choose the wrong god to follow, it could cost you many years and much money before you find out you've been tricked, and in the case of the followers of recent false gods such as Jim Jones, even your very life.

> I freed a thousand slaves. I could have freed a thousand more if only they knew they were slaves.
> ~Harriet Tubman
> (African-American abolitionist, humanitarian, and Union spy during the American Civil War)

Which God Should I Choose?

Although it would be fun to look at where each of these extinct false gods came from and how and when they fell from worship status to historical fiction, it probably would make a lot more sense time-wise to just take a look at some of the gods that are around today. Where they came from, what they offer, and where their followers are headed.

I'm not sure which gods you might be considering right now, but I'll try to cover many of the more prominent ones in the world today and sum it up with what sounds like the best choice.

There is one growing religion (or movement) that teaches we can be our own gods, but I think it's pretty obvious by now that that's not going to work. The life of the average person is a train wreck. Either it's happened, is happening or is about to happen. The ones who buy into this philosophy of becoming your own god are doing pretty well at the time they hear it, so it doesn't sound like such a bad idea. For anyone who has already messed their life up pretty good, becoming your own god doesn't really sound all that genius. The one who is heading for the bottom, or has already hit, and believes they can turn things around by becoming their own god is unfortunately very delusional. After all, who got them where they are in the first place?

It is clear that if we want to get out of the pit we have dug, which we call our life, we are going to have to find a real God that can lead us out of the bondage we're in. Anyone searching for God should understand that He is the God who's going to save them, not one that's just going to bury them deeper in misery. The ideal God to find and follow is the one who has been around since the beginning, created all things, has absolute power over all these things, loves you, and is willing to have a one-on-one relationship with you. That's the God to choose.

Chapter Three

DEADLY CULTS

Tricks and treachery are the practice of fools, that don't have brains enough to be honest.
~Benjamin Franklin (1706-1790)

THE PEOPLES TEMPLE

*C*ults are dangerous on a whole bunch of levels. We have plenty of evidence in recent history to prove beyond a doubt that cults can be a very fatal way to roll. In one way or another, they always end up extracting your life from you physically, spiritually, or both. They have no upside unless you are in leadership, and that is short-lived. Memberships are populated by people who have no understanding whatsoever of what God is really like. They follow a doctrine or teaching of whatever the cult leader makes up and convinces them is true.

Cult leaders are mostly always the same. They may look different from one another, but they all have similar personalities, traits, and characteristics and are as easy to spot as a white bunny in a dog fight. They are self-centered narcissists. They always demand excessive, undivided allegiance to flatter their highly inflated ego. They feel they are entitled to royal treatment and believe, because of their genius, they are capable of unlimited success and are virtually unstoppable. Rules and laws are not meant for them.

They are manipulative and expect their followers to turn over all their money, possessions, and even their children. They have very short, explosive tempers and consider anyone against them as the enemy. They believe themselves to be god, his messiah, or his messenger. Like Satan, they reference themselves as "I" repeatedly, and dominate conversations with talk of themselves. "I" this and "I" that. They are continually paranoid concerning the loyalty of followers and the world around them. They are total control freaks who typically try to isolate their followers from society in remote, secluded compounds or strongholds if possible, and regulate their contact with family and friends. They will use force, such as armed guards or militia-type governance when necessary, to take control of their freedom.

If you happen to wander upon such a person as this, involved in any kind of ministry whatsoever, run. Their charismatic personalities are very attractive and winning. They can lure unsuspecting followers into their belief system quite easily. You will not want to get involved in whatever kind of spirituality this person is promoting or advocating.

At the very least, it will cost you everything you have. Cult leaders may start out rather pathetically with only a handful of followers and, for the most part, seem fairly interesting and harmless. But, as time goes on, they always seem to gain followers, no matter how ludicrous their teachings may be. Over time, however, even as their ministries grow, their mental stability diminishes. Their narcissism escalates to borderline psychotic behavior, and it's in that phase of their degeneracy that very bad things begin to happen.

It's safe to say, I guess, that sometimes people go a little overboard with their gloom and doom hype as they rant about all the bad that's going to happen in various situations, but in the case of religious cults, with all the recent cult fiascoes, there is some credibility here.

For instance, earlier I mentioned a guy named Jim Jones in relation to getting factual information before joining a cult or religion. Reverend James Warren "Jim" Jones was a charismatic leader who founded a cult he called the Peoples Temple in 1956. He continued as the leader of that organization until his death in 1978.

He started his first church in Indianapolis, Indiana, but in 1966 moved his Peoples Temple assembly to Redwood Valley, California due to an investigation into his fake healing services. In his healing services, he produced animal parts, such as chicken livers, that he said were cancerous tumors he had removed from his victims.

He chose this city because of a vision he claimed to have had of a nuclear attack on Chicago that would also destroy Indianapolis. He had recently read an article naming Redwood as one of the least likely places to get hit in a nuclear attack. As hard as it is to imagine, sixty-five families made the move with him from Indiana to California.

With his roots now planted in California, Jim Jones began to experience great success. He eventually established locations in over twelve California cities, including San Francisco and Los Angeles. At the height of his ministry, the Peoples Temple boasted of 20,000 members, although conservative figures support more between 3,000 and 5,000. Members or not, the San Francisco location alone drew 3,000 attendees to each meeting. I should point out that their standard method of operation was going around to different cities, bringing members with them who posed as locals and pretended to be healed in public healing meetings.

Jones had an intense phobia regarding the American government, specifically the FBI and CIA, as well as the media and its constant probing into his affairs. He was also abnormally concerned with defectors, for which he actually sent out search parties to track down, even renting airplanes to scour highways.

Subsequently, as his ministry in California grew, his paranoia, enhanced by excessive drug abuse, began to spiral out of control. In order to avoid exposure of his questionable practices, which had now escalated beyond fake healing services to drug abuse, tax evasion, misappropriation of funds, involvement with the Symbianese Liberation Army, and the suspicious death of the husband of a recent defector, Jones fled from California to Guyana. There, on rented land, he began to build a colony called the Peoples Temple Agricultural Project, dubbed "Jonestown." From 1974 to 1977, there were as few as fifty inhabitants, but by promising followers tropical paradise and freedom from the world's evil, by late 1978, he had managed to persuade over 900 people to join him at his colony.

During his years in California, Jim Jones had begun to believe that he was the Christ, and now, during the last three years of his life in Jonestown, God Himself.

Amid reports of inhabitants being abused and held there against their will, San Francisco Congressman Leo Ryan flew to Jonestown to investigate the allegations. During his visit, several people approached Ryan, fearful for their lives and wanting to leave the compound. On November 17, 1978, Congressman Ryan and several defectors reached the airstrip, which was about six miles from Jonestown at a small town called Port Kaituma. While boarding two small planes, temple security guards opened fire on the group, killing Congressman Ryan and four others. This massacre of innocent victims marked the beginning of the sudden end of Jim Jones and his Peoples Temple.

> "Ignorance breeds monsters to fill up the vacancies of the soul that are unoccupied by the verities of knowledge."
> ~Horace Mann (1796–1859)

In most instances, the powder keg won't blow unless someone lights the fuse. The powder keg in this instance was called the Peoples Temple, which was a very unstable group who regularly rehearsed taking poison together as a trial run for what Jones referred to as "revolutionary suicide." Members would line up to receive grape Flavor Aid, which everyone was ordered to drink. They were told that they would die in about forty-five minutes. At the end of that time, Jones would announce that they had not really ingested poison, but were taking part in a loyalty test. Each time, he did sternly warn them, though, that they would soon have to take the poison for real.

You might wonder where they would get enough poison for a thousand people. To accomplish this, Jones had obtained a jeweler's license that allowed him to import a half pound of cyanide monthly for nearly two years under the pretense of cleaning gold. On the final day, they mixed the cyanide with grape Flavor Aid in a large vat with such drugs as liquid valium, penegram and chloral hydrate.

I doubt many of them were anxious to commit suicide as a way out, but options were thin. Jones at least believed it would be a good way to teach the world a lesson and get his point across. He had also started to develop a theory that he called "translation" whereby he and his followers, upon their mass suicide together, would be transported to another world of Shangri la. By this time, Jones' mental state had severely deteriorated to the point where he was slurring his words and not finishing sentences. After long mandatory workdays, inhabitants of Jonestown were subjected to lengthy communist seminars and recordings made by Jones of lessons and news reports that he had played over loud speakers throughout the colony all night long.

It is unknown how long they may have continued existing there at Jonestown, if left to themselves. Possibly indefinitely, but Congressman Ryan's visit and subsequent murder proved to be the unraveling of the fragile cord that held this group together.

After Jones' hit squad, which he called the "Red Brigade," finished their mission, they returned to the colony that night where the preparations for the end had been made ready. Workers had already prepared a vat of poison-laced grape Flavor Aid at the main pavilion. A death tape recording of the events of that night is available if you wish to know more, but it suffices to say that the 276 children who died that night did not kill themselves. Mothers used syringes without needles to squirt the poison into the mouths of their babies and older children. Some people, apparently having second thoughts, were held down and injected with poison or shot, while most of the remaining 914 people who perished there that night obediently drank their drink and waited to die. Some ran into the jungle to escape or hid under huts until everyone else was dead.[1]

THE BRANCH DAVIDIANS

Hateful to me as the gates of Hades is that man who hides one thing in his heart and speaks another.
~Homer (800 BC–701 BC)

Another notable recent cult disaster culminated in 1993 at a compound located just outside Waco, Texas. Although the roots of this cult go back as far as 1929 with the formation of the Seventh-day Adventist church (and that the group consisted of one heretic after another), we will pick up the story in 1984 when Vernon Wayne Howell (later known as David Koresh) began to gain followers in the organization that formed from a schism in 1955 that called themselves the Davidian Seventh-day Adventists. Howell (Koresh) had previously been excommunicated from a Seventh-day Adventist Church for his immoral actions involving the fifteen-year-old daughter of the church's pastor.

Howell had tried to infiltrate this sect, more commonly known as the Branch Davidians, who operated the compound near Waco, called Mount Carmel Center, without success between 1981 and 1983. In 1983, however, he was given permission to speak his views and at that point, began to gain a following. Through military-style assaults on the Mount Carmel Center and heavily manipulated court proceedings, Vernon Wayne Howell, now known as David Koresh, seems to have gained control of the Mount Carmel compound by 1988. He named his group the "Davidian Branch Davidian Seventh-day Adventist Association."

From then until his death in 1993, the situation at Mount Carmel deteriorated to exactly what you would expect to find when a diabolical, narcissistic, psychopathic pedophile gains control of an organization and convinces people that he has been sent by God.

In February of 1993, amid accusations and evidence of automatic weapons stockpiling, child abuse, and statutory rape, the Federal Bureau of Alcohol, Tobacco, and Firearms staged a raid on Mount Carmel. The residents resisted the ATF agents' attempt to execute their search warrant, at which point a vicious, two-hour-long gun battle broke out that claimed the lives of four ATF agents and six Branch Davidian members. At that point, due to, among other things, the deaths of four federal agents, the FBI initiated a siege of the Mount Carmel compound.

Although the main concern of the ATF was the compelling evidence that the Branch Davidians were stockpiling illegal automatic weapons, they attempted to serve their warrant the day after the *Waco Tribune-Herald* reported that Koresh had physically abused children inside the compound, and had fathered at least a dozen children through a harem of wives, some as young as twelve or thirteen years old at the time of their marriage to him. According to the report, he believed he was entitled to as many as 140 wives and could take any females from the group he chose and have them as his own.

The FBI continued their siege of the compound for the next fifty-one days, and although twenty-one children and up to fourteen adults had been released by negotiation, eighty-five people, including David Koresh and as many as twenty-three children, remained inside the compound.

On the fifty-first day of the siege, April 19, 1993, at 6:00 AM, the FBI launched a tear gas raid on the building that housed the members, in an attempt to flush out the Davidians without harming anyone. After six hours of tear gas assault, no one had left the building, and at around noon, three fires broke out in different areas of the compound. Nine people escaped the fire. The remaining seventy-six people, including twenty-three children, all died. It was reported that members were prevented from leaving the burning building at first, and eventually became trapped. Those who did not die as a result of the fire died of gunshot wounds, presumably at the hands of other members.

It is interesting to note, for the followers anyway, that during hostage negotiations with the FBI, David Koresh declined numerous opportunities for everyone to walk out of the compound unharmed. Koresh informed negotiators that he was the second coming of Christ, and his father in Heaven had told him to remain inside the compound. This pretty much sealed the fate of the followers of David Koresh, whether they wanted to stay and die or not.[2]

HEAVEN'S GATE

> You can fool some of the people all the time, and all of the people some of the time, but you cannot fool all of the people all the time.
> ~Abraham Lincoln (1809-1865)

Okay, this group is going to seem a little weird to most people, and, although it does sound kind of humorous when you examine the facts underlying their beliefs, it is still tragic that people can be persuaded to take their own lives in pursuit of God, or in this case, I guess, Heaven.

Founders Marshall Applewhite and Bonnie Nettles modified their beliefs over time and underwent several name changes before finally settling on the name

Which God Should I Choose?

Heaven's Gate. Applewhite was a UFO-type cultist, believing that spacemen (ancient astronauts) had come to the earth, leaving the first humans here, and would soon be coming back to collect a chosen few. He believed that aliens spoke to him through the Star Trek TV series.[3] What they said, I can only guess.

Nettles, on the other hand was a psychic follower who often met with fortunetellers and conducted séances in order to talk with dead spirits. She teamed up with Applewhite in 1972, and the pair began to believe, or at least teach their followers, that they were the two witnesses whose coming was foretold in the book of Revelation, a Bible book, and that they were aliens.[4]

As far as the two witnesses in the Bible go, that would be a neat trick, since among other things these two witnesses will have the ability to kill their enemies with fire that comes from their mouths and turn the earth's waters into blood. Clearly, if you had read the book of Revelation, you would have known Applewhite and Nettles were not these two.

As far as being aliens, after the notion of "walk ins" became popular in the 1970s, they changed their story a little and began teaching that they were "extraterrestrial walk- ins."

A walk-in can be defined as "an entity who occupies a body that has been vacated by its original soul."[5] Probably not surprisingly, modern-day psychiatrists, mental health professionals, and even philosophers categorize this belief system as nonsense. But, when a good salesman is selling something that he believes in, others sometimes buy in.

In addition to the alien/UFO backdrop of their teaching, Applewhite and Nettles also believed that in order to make themselves worthy of the next life, or next level as they called it, members had to completely give up all ties to this world including their family, friends, sexuality, individuality, jobs, money, and possessions, and to hate all aspects of this world.[6]

They believed that their bodies were a "vehicle" that their spirit was using on its journey from one level to the next. Around 1996, Applewhite began teaching that the earth was about to be "recycled," or wiped clean, and the only way for their spirits to survive this apocalypse would be to get out quick. So, it only made sense, when an amateur astronomer reported he had discovered a spaceship following the Hale-Bopp[7] comet in November, 1996, that Heaven's Gate leader Marshall Applewhite determined that their ride to the next level had arrived. This was their "next vehicle."[8]

But, he surmised, in order to reach this "next vehicle" they would have to kill the vehicle they were living in now. This would set their spirits free so they'd be able to rendezvous with their new ride out of here. Applewhite was apparently against suicide, but is quoted as saying, "It was the only way to evacuate this Earth." So, he and thirty-eight members, in three groups, ingested Phenobarbital, cyanide, and arsenic mixed with applesauce or pudding and placed plastic bags over their heads in order to asphyxiate themselves.[9]

Because of the nature of this group, it is doubtful even with proper warning that the ones involved in this cult could have been persuaded to avoid their ill fate. In fact, a couple of members who were not present during the suicide carnage later both committed suicide themselves, even though the comet was gone and their friends were all dead. It had to be obvious at that point that there was no spaceship to begin with, and that these people all died for nothing. Their leader had been so persuasive though, that they believed in him and his off-the-wall teachings without question.

Which God Should I Choose?

This cult is included in this section, not because droves of people will fall prey to a UFO cult, but because it goes to show that religious cults come in many different shapes and sizes, and all are equally as dangerous.

It is possible, however, that you or someone you know may be involved in or considering a similar UFO-type cult. Although the concept of UFOs can be intriguing, it should never be taken seriously.

> I cannot teach anybody anything. I can only make them think.
> ~Socrates (469 BC-399 BC)

Consider the facts. The nearest star and *possible* Solar System (we do not know if it even has any planets) to ours is nearly five light years away, or 25.8 trillion miles. The fastest spacecraft that we have developed to date, called New Horizons, could travel there in about 78,000 years. It has been proposed that superior technology could develop a nuclear or ion-powered spaceship that could reach much higher speeds and therefore get there from here sooner. The problem with that, among many others, is that it would require an area equivalent to that of ten super tankers just for fuel storage (each one at least three times bigger than Noah's Ark). That's roughly 20 million barrels or 840 million gallons worth of volume or total tank size of 2,500 feet wide by 15,000 feet long by 1,400 feet tall. And that's just the size of the fuel tank.[10]

The numerous sightings of UFOs in the last sixty years has made many believers, but what the believers in aliens don't realize is that each UFO would require a fuel tank the size of five Empire State buildings to get here—plus, they would have to refuel in order to get home. Can you imagine how big five Empire State buildings would be? Since we have no such fuel to lend, there would be thousands and thousands (based on reported sightings) of spaceships sitting or floating around, out of fuel (each one bigger than five Empire State Buildings lumped together). In addition, the crew members would have to be capable of living to be several thousand years old, not eat much for those several thousand years, and not move around a whole lot either. When you have the facts, it seems like it would be far easier to believe in the God who says He created all of these stars that are trillions of miles away, all on the same day, both to light up our night sky and prove to observers who He is.

Someone may suggest to you that Mars, which is much closer, would be a spot that aliens could easily travel from. It is true that many people have, and many people do believe in the possibility of the existence of Martians. There are some major problems to be aware of in relation to finding life on Mars. The average daily temperature on Mars is minus 55 degrees Fahrenheit. Some days it actually drops to minus 225 degrees Fahrenheit—that's 225 degrees below zero.

Add to this the fact that there is no water, only traces of oxygen, and month-long, planet-wide dust storms, and you can imagine quite easily that sustaining life under these conditions is somewhat doubtful. Building a spacecraft in an environment like this would be absolutely impossible.[11]

I was in Inlet, New York, in the early 1990s when the temperature dropped overnight to minus 42 degrees Fahrenheit. When I went out at 6:00 AM, first of all, it is hard to explain what the cold felt like at 42 below, but then, when I turned the key, my van made a faint *"wumph"* noise and then was silent. I went back in the house, where it took an hour to get warm again. The temperature I experienced that day was warmer than the average daily temperature on Mars. Later, a neighbor told me that the temperature had dropped to minus 52 degrees Fahrenheit at Inlet/Old Forge, New York, in 1979. Her husband and brothers were loggers back then, and she said that it took them the whole day to get all of their equipment started. When they finally did, it was time to shut down and head home.

The bottom line is this. No aliens are coming. As far as we know, God did not create them. It's just another smokescreen to lead us farther away from the true God. We should never proceed on, or believe in, speculation of things that cannot be proven. It will always lead us in the wrong direction, without fail. We must always draw our conclusions from the proof of the evidence presented if we are to find our way to the right God.

Although the chances of any of us falling prey to this kind of deception is somewhat remote, reviewing the goings-ons of these cults that have ended in disaster provide us with several very good reasons why we should have all the facts before we decide which god we should follow. Even if it's not so off-the-wall as aliens coming to take us away, it could be a more credible-sounding cult or religion that was formed through the misguided visions of angels or false prophets that are far less crazy-sounding and dancing more closely to the truth.

There are those who can capture others quite easily with their charm, stage presence and apparent strengths. They prey on people who are looking for a god to follow and don't have the proper information or warning. It is vitally important that we be made aware of these underhanded schemers because these kinds of people exist in our world today by the boatload and are actively seeking followers. In your quest to find God, avoid these kinds of people and their organizations like the plague.

There are plenty of Jim Jones, David Koresh and Marshall Applewhite types all around us whose dealings we need to be informed about so we can make the right choice and choose the right God.

There are also some religions and cults in existence that may not seem all that bad upon first glance. They have been around a long time and have never really had a disaster like the ones mentioned in this chapter. Their leaders seem normal and their followers look like average, everyday people. The problem remains, if they are not following the right God, and continue following a false god that is leading them away from the real God, eventually they will come to a place where they find that everything they have known was a lie and they have ended up wasting the lives that the real God has given them. If they do not discover the truth before they die, then they will be standing before God in the judgment and at that point will have no opportunity to undo the eternal mistake they have made.

That's why it is so vitally important to do your homework on God. Research all you possibly can from accepted reference books. By accepted, I mean you need to determine, starting with the truths you glean from this book, which writers are teaching about the real God, and start reading their work. There are myriads of books written about the real God that will help you learn more about Him and grow closer to Him. As you begin to know God, you will be able to tell more easily whose teaching you should be listening to and whose you should not. If a teacher's words don't line up with what we know to be true about God, then he or she is a false teacher. All false teachers should be avoided whenever possible because they will confuse you and can actually lead you away from God rather than the intended result of growing closer to Him. I will give you some definite places to start looking for true teaching at the end of this book. The teachers I recommend will help you to grow in the grace and knowledge of God.

Seek Him, therefore, with all your heart and you will find Him. It is a verifiable fact that wise men went searching for Him over 2,000 years ago. There's a catchy little saying you may have heard that says, "Wise men still seek Him today." I will add to that, wise women do as well.

These are some of the more physically dangerous cults of the recent past. However, there are quite a few current cults in operation that are not so dangerous physically (at least for now), but are still extremely dangerous spiritually. We will go over a few of these as well as take a brief look at some of today's more prominent religions.

Chapter Four

ATTRACTIVE ARTICULATE

JEHOVAH'S WITNESSES

Fifty years ago, there were less than 100,000 known Jehovah's Witnesses. Today, there are over 7 million members of this cult around the world. Jehovah's Witnesses are by far one of the most active groups in sharing their beliefs of any known religious organization. After all, who has not seen two or three well-dressed, respectable looking people walking or driving around the neighborhood with Bibles in their hands?

Their message is clear, and they have what appears to be a Bible to back up all of their beliefs and teachings. The book they refer to as a bible, however, is strictly a private translation that drastically distorts the actual original Scriptures.

The Jehovah's Witnesses' beliefs were devised and developed by Charles Taze Russell between 1870 and 1916. Russell wrote a series of six books called the *Millennial Dawn*.[12] After Russell's death in 1916, his successor J.F. Rutherford wrote the seventh and final volume of the series. The controversial message of this series spread through the cooperation and aid of the Watch Tower Bible and Tract Society, but because their beliefs were so far removed from the Bible, they did not attract overwhelming numbers of followers.

This all changed when in 1961 the Jehovah's Witnesses published their own bible translation called the New World Translation. This translation altered the entire message of the Bible to match the teachings of Russell and Rutherford, combined with the teachings of their successors that had evolved within the cult up until that time. Now, with a bible in their hand to authenticate their message, they attracted new followers in significant numbers.[13]

There are numerous books and websites that deal with the errors that are woven throughout this translation. I encourage you to check these errors out if you are now involved with or have been considering the Jehovah's Witnesses as representatives of the true God. Clearly, after examining the evidence, you will see that they are not.

Remember, one of the compelling indicators of a false religion or false god is if they take an already-established truth and change it to suit their needs.

It should be proof enough just to consider that the entire doctrine of the Jehovah's Witnesses was developed between 1870 and 1961, and then is endorsed by a private bible translation that matches and supports *their* personally devised doctrinal beliefs alone.

When I was teenager playing cards with my friends, we referred to this ploy as stacking the deck. The Jehovah's Witnesses cult is actually a new twist on an old game. A game that you will not want to get involved with if you are trying to choose the right God.

CHRISTIAN SCIENCE

Of all the cults, Christian Science is probably the most inappropriately named due to the fact that it is not a Christian organization and its beliefs hold no scientific truth. Numbers of members of this cult have been dwindling over the years for what seem like realistic reasons.

Christian Science thinking originated with the teachings of Mary Baker Eddy in 1866. After a serious supposed fatal accident, she began reading the Bible. On the third day, she rose from her bed healed. She believed that God revealed to her a mind over matter healing process that Jesus supposedly used, that was spawned through prayer. In 1875, she published a book outlining this spiritual healing process called *Science and Health*. In 1879, this "teaching" was given the name Christian Science.[14]

Like many Eastern religions, Christian Science teaches that God and all else are only spiritual. Matter only exists as an illusion in our minds and is only overcome by reaching an understanding of this fact. They teach that if we believe that matter is real, then we will be subject to it. If we come to an understanding that matter (including our bodies) is an illusion, we begin to be freed from the physical laws that govern them, and this leads to physical healing through spiritual belief.

If Christian Science is mixed with any other belief system or physical remedy, such as medicine, healing will not occur. Numerous testimonies of members who prayed for healing and received it have drawn converts into this cult in the past, but today, with so many advancements in medical technology and science that were not available at the time of Mary Baker Eddy, more and more people are becoming perfectly aware that matter is real, and if we wait too long to seek medical attention, we may regress beyond the point of healing.

Members of this religion meet regularly to share healing experiences and even read Bible passages as part of their meetings. Since their beliefs stray so far from the Bible's teachings, it would be better to find an organization that adheres strictly to the Bible's message if you are even remotely considering choosing the God of the Bible to be your God.

Chapter Five

FROM NEAR TO FAR EAST, TO WEST, BY SOUTHEAST ASIA

*I*t's hard to get a handle on who's who in religions these days, because there are so many in so many different places. There are a lot of world's biggest religions lists with different religions and beliefs taking different positions on those lists. But, for the most part, you can get twenty or so in a group that seems to have more followers than anyone else. Of those twenty, there are ten established religions that probably top the list of the estimated 730 organized religions in the world today. They are considered the top ten due to the estimated numbers of so-called followers.

Christianity tops the list with approximately 2.3 billion followers which constitute about 32 percent of the world's population. It has been a few years since new figures have been compiled, but it is estimated that Christianity grows at about the same rate as the population. Islam is close behind with 1.6 billion, which is about 23 percent of the world's population, while Hinduism, with nearly 1 billion followers, represents 15 percent. Although Islam and Hinduism have smaller followings, they are growing at a slightly higher rate than Christianity. Islam's higher growth rate may be in part to its estimated growth rate of 80 percent among prison inmates who turn to faith while in prison. We will discuss that a little further in the section dealing with Islam.

Buddhism, which seems like it should be bigger, has less than half the followers of Hinduism with 376 million followers or 6 percent of the world's population. Of the remaining organized religions in the world, none contain more than 1 percent each of the world's population. Some of the bigger of these smaller religions are Sikhism which has 23 million followers, Judaism with 14 million, Bahaism with 7 million, Confusionism with 6.3 million, Jainism with 4.2 million and Shinto with 4 million.[14]

We will take a brief look at some of these religions to see if they warrant any further attention, along with some of the more popular "fringe" religions, or cults, that many people are at least a little curious about. Some of the major ones listed above may have surprised you if you're anything like me, because up until recently, I had never even heard of them.

NEAR EAST

BAHAISM

Bahaism, a religion that emphasizes spiritual unity and peace, was, somewhat ironically, founded in Iran in 1863 by Baha'ullah. With an estimated 7 million followers, it is nearly twice the size of Shinto or Jainism, or roughly the same size as both of these combined.

Born Husayn-'Ali at Teheran, Iran in 1817, he changed his name to Baha'ullah which means "the glory of God" in Arabic, during his four month incarceration in Teheran's Black Pit prison.[15] After his release, he spent the next forty years producing thousands of books, tablets, and letters which today form the core of the of Baha'i faith beliefs.

These beliefs include that throughout history, god has revealed himself to mankind through a series of divine messengers, whose teachings guide and educate us and provide the basis for the advancement of human society. These messengers have included Abraham, Krishna, Zoroaster, Moses, Buddha, Jesus, and Muhammad. Their religions come from the same source and are in essence successive chapters of one religion from God.[16]

I have to pause here and interject that nothing could be further from the truth. Many of the people on this list are as far apart in beliefs and teachings as the night is from the day. At least one was a murderer, one didn't even believe in God, and only a few on this list believed in heaven and hell.

> If there is no Hell, a good many preachers are obtaining money under false pretences.
> ~William A. Sunday (1862-1935)

As followers of Baha'ullah, Baha'is recognize him as the manifestation of god for our time — the promised one of all religions. He is, in their eyes, the Spirit of Truth of Christianity, the Al-Maseeh of Islam, the Maitreya Buddha of Buddhism, the Shah Brahram of Zoroastrianism, the Messiah ben David of Judaism and the Kalki Avatar of Vaishnavism. It's no wonder they have 7 million followers. They've invited people from all religions and promised them a world of peace with their own god ruling over it. All this sounds like wishful thinking, and unfortunately, for reasons mentioned previously (plus many others), it's just not true.

It's fair to say that Baha'ullah, who thought he was the latest of these messengers sent to bring new spiritual and social teachings for his time, had a really good plan and a true desire for world unity. His teaching of the oneness of god, the oneness of the human family, and the oneness of religion shows that he was seeking a one-world religion where all people would worship the same god together in peace.

Baha'ullah said, "The earth is but one country and mankind its citizens," and that, as foretold in all the sacred scriptures of the past, "now is the time for humanity to live in unity."

Founded more than a century and a half ago, the Baha'i faith has spread around the globe. Members of the Baha'i faith live in more than 100,000 localities and come from nearly every nation, ethnic group, culture, profession, and social or economic background.

Baha'i believes the crucial need facing humanity is to find a unifying vision of the nature and purpose of life and of the future of society. Such a vision unfolds in the writings of Baha'ullah.[17]

Although this all sounds good on the surface, what we're talking about here is a better life on earth, with absolutely no vision for the future beyond more wishful thinking.

> Aim at heaven, and you will get earth thrown in; aim at earth, and you will get neither.
> ~C. S. Lewis, Irish author and scholar
> (1898-1963)

If you dig deep enough, you will get to the truth of the matter. Baha'i does not believe in heaven or hell. At least they don't believe that they are literal places, but conditions of the soul. Baha'ullah taught that when we die, we go on to the next world. He said, "If our souls have the condition of Heaven then the next world will appear as Heaven. If our soul in this life is in the condition of Hell then the next world will appear as Hell. What Heaven and Hell are actually like we cannot know in this life; just like a child in the womb can't understand what mortal life is like until it is experienced."

This statement is completely false because if there is a heaven and a hell, they are literal, physical places and we can know exactly what they are like and what it takes to obtain residence in either one of them. The record of the creation of heaven and hell is first given to us in the Bible. Any change or difference from the original record has got to be a lie. There is no other place that they were mentioned beforehand and no one ever knew of the existence of anything like them until they were first recorded in the Bible. So, if you believe there is a heaven or a hell, then the Bible is the place you must look to get the original, truthful details and information. Since there is no prior account, and this account is considered historically correct by all of the accepted criteria for true history, then this account has got to be the truth. Remember, truth is the absence of all lies, not just some of them. If there are some lies, then the whole thing is a lie.

ISLAM

> Every violation of truth is not only a sort of suicide in the liar, but is a stab at the health of human society.
> ~Ralph Waldo Emerson (1803-1882)

Islam is the second largest religion in the world, and one of the fastest growing. Its founder is Halabi, later known as Muhammad. Halabi was born in Mecca, Saudi Arabia, in 570 AD. He began attracting followers, including his cousin and son-in-law, Ali, about 610 AD, after several instances of hearing voices that he eventually came to believe was the angel Gabriel.[18]

Although the area of Mecca was saturated with idols, Halabi, now called Muhammad, began to teach that Allah was the only real god. Allah was the god of the local Quarish tribe that Muhammad belonged to before he invented Islam. Islam was designed to lead his people out of their worship of many gods and idols. The Qur'an says that Muhammad drove the other idols away and made Allah the only god, and he, Muhammad, was his messenger. According to Al-Vaqqidi (a Muslim biographer of Mohammad and a historian of Islam), Allah was actually Hubal, the chief of the 360 gods being worshipped in Arabia at the time Muhammad rose to prominence. History points toward Hubal as the moon god that Arabs worshipped at the Kaa'ba and used the name *Allah* when they prayed.[19] According to the Encyclopedia of Religion, Hubal was a statue likeness of a man whose body was made of red precious stones and whose arms were made of gold.[20]

The Kaa'ba shrine in Mecca was formerly named Beit-Allah meaning, House of Allah. It housed a black stone which measures eleven inches by fifteen inches, which is believed to have fallen from heaven. This belief predates Islam. Muhammad kept the Kaa'ba as a holy, sacred place and confirmed that the black stone had the power to take away man's sins.

Followers of Islam are known as Muslims, which means "one who submits." As part of their submission, known as the five pillars of Islam, every able-bodied, traditional Muslim (Sunni) who can afford to do so must make a hajj, or pilgrimage to Mecca at least once in their lifetime.

The other four Sunni pillars include the testimony of faith (Shahada) which they must recite upon conversion to Islam and then again every day in their prayers. The Shahada states that there is only one god, and Muhammad is his only prophet. Also, they must perform five ritual prayers (salat) every day, give a percentage of their wealth once a year (zakat) and fast (sawm—refrain from eating or drinking) from dawn to sunset during the ninth month of the Islamic calendar.

Not all of the many divisions of Islam hold to these five tenets and have devised their own sets of rules. There are in fact over 150 sects of Muslims. The largest group, called Sunni, constitute about 90 percent of all Muslims. The other main divisions are the Shiites (the second largest group), Wahhabis, Suffis, and the Baha'is.[21]

> Falsehood is never so successful as when she baits her hook with truth, and no opinions so fatally mislead us, as those that are not wholly wrong; as no watches so effectually deceive the wearer as those that are sometimes right.
> ~Charles Caleb Colton (1780-1832)

Islam is a seriously complicated religion. On one hand, you have over a billion peaceful followers of Islam divided up in over 150 branches. On the other hand, The National Counterterrorism Center (NCTC), which was established by Presidential Executive Order 13354 in August, 2004, found that for the last three years the largest percentage of terrorist attacks in the world were perpetrated by Sunni Muslims.

The NCTC reported that in 2011 there were 10,283 terrorist attacks around the globe resulting in 12,533 deaths. Of these attacks, 56 percent of the attacks and 70 percent of the fatalities were attributed to Sunni Muslims. However, even if CNN's Glenn Beck is correct and 10 percent of all Muslims are terrorists, that still leaves nearly a billion followers that are at least somewhat peaceful.[22]

There are numerous red flags that pop up as we study this religion, its origin, its books, and its beliefs that have to become a major concern if we are hoping to make the right choice. When you have to ask, "Is it peaceful?" or "Is it terrorist?" then that right there is enough to say we should probably be looking someplace else to find the real God, who is characterized by love. There are several verses in Islamic writings that would lead you to believe that there may be something to all the negative articles that have been written about this religion. Of course, Muslim sympathizers have plenty of other verses to counter these, so looking at verses alone will probably not be enough to ensure you make the right decision on this one.

Among other negatives are the troubling reports from multiple sources concerning the staggering amount of prison inmates around the world who are becoming Muslims. As many as 80 percent of all prisoners who turn to faith in prison are choosing Islam. Turning to faith is not as concerning as the reasons given for this trend. Prisoners are often coerced to become Muslims in order to receive safety, better food, better living conditions, and preferential treatment. Even more alarming is the evidence that Muslim prison converts are being actively recruited as future extremists, which is making prisons, among other things, active breeding grounds for radicals (terrorists).

We need to be careful here though, because terrorism and peace are not the issue for us as we are trying to decide which god we should choose. We shouldn't be looking for a peaceful religion any more than we should be looking for a violent one. If we hope to find the right God, then we have to go back to the facts that deal with God in order to learn the truth about Him, and not the religions or the religious teachings of men.

In chapter twelve, which deals with Judaism, we will see that there are multiple associations between these two religions (Judaism and Islam) found in their writings which rightly attest to the fact that there can only be one God. There are, however, vast verifiable differences between the two which prove that only one of them can be true and they definitely represent two completely different gods.

Chapter Six

FAR EAST

SHINTO

Shinto is possibly the tenth largest religion in the world today with officially 3 to 4 million adherents. Unofficially, several estimates place its total membership as high as 118 million. That's a lot of people, but for the most part, they are all Japanese. I'm including it here, one, because of its size, and two, I'm hoping a number of Japanese people may read this book.

Shinto's beginnings can be traced back to at least the sixth century AD. It is a predominantly Japanese religion that was founded in Japan and, for the most part, deals with Japan. Shinto teaches that no other land is divine but Japan, making Japan uniquely special in the world. It teaches that Japan's islands were the first land to be created and as such, are to be considered paradise.

Shintos believe that Japan is the country of the gods and the Japanese people themselves are descendants of gods. This, then, gives Shintoists a certain conviction of superiority over other countries and people.

For the most part, Shinto has no named leader or founder, no sacred writings, or any authoritative set of beliefs. A major aspect of Shinto is the philosophy of kami, the concept of sacred power in both animate and inanimate objects. In the Shinto religion, there is a powerful sense of the presence of gods and spirits in nature. Worship of these gods takes place at one of the numerous shrines scattered throughout the country of Japan, although many Japanese have altars in their homes devoted to one or more of the large number of Shinto gods.[23]

Unless you are Japanese or at least live in Japan, Shinto is probably not on your list of possible religions to pursue. If you have considered it though, bear in mind that most of the tenets of this religion go against the grain of what we should be looking for when choosing the right God. Some of the more obvious red flags that pop up would be that the whole Shinto belief system has only been around since the sixth century AD, there is more than one god involved, and the people are taught that they are the descendants of gods.

Remember, when trying to decide which God we should choose, we should be looking for a God who is the One and only God and is the creator of all things. People of the real God would be part of His creation, not His descendants.

CONFUCIANISM

Confucianism is one religion that I didn't want to leave out because I imagine almost everyone has heard of it. When I was a kid, we would go around all the time saying "Confucius say" and then share some witty anecdote related to whatever incident we happened to be involved in.

In reality, Confucius, who was born and lived in China from 551 to 479 BC, was a pretty interesting guy. He was a very smart philosopher and thinker who spoke at least 219 wise, mixed-with-practical sayings which are recorded in a book called *Analects* that are often quoted and have deeply influenced Chinese culture and beyond for the past 2,500 years.

Actually, Confucianism is not really a religion at all, but more an ethical system that deals mainly with a person's moral conduct and ethical behavior. This would not be a bad thing, except that he also taught that these virtues could come to a person from within themselves, rather than from God.

Confucius believed and taught that man is capable of doing all that is necessary to improve his life and his culture through his own self effort, drawing on the goodness within himself to pull it off.

In essence, it sounds a lot like the modern philosophy of today that teaches you can be your own god and take control of your own life. In reality, that is romantic supposition at best. I know even a blind squirrel finds a nut once in a while, but expecting that people are going to be able to change their lives from evil to good on their own is a delusional presumption. Whole cultures are disintegrating all around us while philosophers teach that we're evolving into perfect creatures and we can call on our innermost beings to repair the damage we have done to ourselves.

In spite of this, it is estimated that there are over 6 million followers of Confucius. It's hard to establish for sure just how many followers there really are because it is possible to be a Buddhist or Shintoist and still be a follower of Confucius.

Confucius was another of those who put their emphasis on the here and now rather than on the hereafter. He believed in ancestor worship and that the spirits of your dead ancestors controlled your fortunes, so you had better be respectful of your elder family members now because they would probably die first.

Which God Should I Choose?

From the teachings of Confucius, we can ascertain that he did not allow for any reliance on God, and from some of the written sayings ascribed to him by his followers, he may not have believed in God at all.

It is true that everybody likes a wise saying. Wise sayings, however, are not going to cure what's wrong, and they are not going to save anybody.

When I was growing up, my best friend was being raised by his grandmother. She had many, many wise sayings, and my friend would actually quote them to me time and time again over the ten years of our friendship.

After high school, we separated and I didn't see him again until we were twenty. He was at that time a shell of the person I knew and remembered. His mind was completely wasted by drug and alcohol consumption and he sat staring straight ahead, thinking of nothing to say.

Fifteen years after that, I bumped into his sister who told me he had become a complete and total burnout. He had no mind left. And then, last year I heard that he died, only making it to his mid fifties.

I still think about all those wise sayings I used to hear him tell, as he was usually correcting me for some form of delinquent behavior I was performing. Unfortunately, without God's help, even the wisest of sayings didn't help me then, and like my friend, will do me no good in the end.

Chapter Seven

SOUTHEAST ASIA

JAINISM

There are at least 4.2 million followers of Jainism, which is another one of the top ten religions by size in the world. This seems incredible due to the extreme forms of asceticism (self-denial) that they practice. Jainism is a highly legalistic religion that teaches you can only attain your salvation through complete self-denial. It is one of the religions I mentioned earlier that has no god. It is a system of beliefs and practices that, in the end, really leads to no defined place.

Jainism also began around the sixth century AD (like Shinto) as a reformation movement within Hinduism. Unlike Shinto, it was founded in India. It is based on the teachings of its founder, Mahavira. Mahavira believed that a life of bitter self-denial was the way to achieve "enlightenment." As part of his own self-denial he wandered around India naked for twelve years, suffering hardship and abuse. He believed one should live their life without harming any other life, which is called the vow of Ahimsa. So, he swept the path in front of him as he walked and strained his water that he drank so as not to kill any bugs or germs. Some Jain monks even wear a cloth over their mouths to prevent accidental harm to airborne germs and insects.[24]

The Jain text of Kalpasutra describes Mahavira's asceticism in detail, from whom most of the ascetic practices are derived as follows: "The Venerable Ascetic Mahavira for a year and a month wore clothes; after that time he walked about naked, and accepted the alms in the hollow of his hand. For more than twelve years the Venerable Ascetic Mahavira neglected his body and abandoned the care of it; he with equanimity bore, underwent, and suffered all pleasant or unpleasant occurrences arising from divine powers, men, or animals" (Kalpa Sutra 117). [25]

Even though Mahavira was willing to deny himself any luxury, he still must have been a very stubborn man because he refused to acknowledge or worship any god. In fact, he adamantly denied that any God or gods existed. According to Jain writings, Mahavira descended from heaven, committed no sin himself, and through meditation, freed himself from all earthly desires.

As per the Jain vows, monks and nuns renounce all relations and possessions. They actually have the best chance at salvation since common citizens normally can only adhere to the first three of the five Jain vows. In order to achieve salvation or enlightenment, you must strictly observe these "Five Great Vows" which, when translated into English, sound very familiar. You must not kill, you must not lie, you should not be greedy, take part in sexual immorality, or have any worldly attachments.

Also, women are to be avoided entirely because they are thought to be the cause of all kinds of evil.[26] The worldly attachments and women vows (four and five) are the ones that catch most of the followers. Only the monks and nuns are very good at obtaining separation from these last two things. Jain monks and nuns practice complete celibacy. They do not touch or even share a sitting platform with a person of the opposite sex.

Jain monks and nuns are nearly possession-less and without any attachment. They travel constantly from city to city, are always barefoot and often cross forests and even deserts to reach their destination. Jain ascetics do not stay in a single place for more than two months in order to prevent attachment to any area. Mahavira himself did not stay in one place any longer than a day.

For possessions, they own only unstitched white robes (an upper and lower garment) and a bowl used for eating and collecting alms. Male Digambara monks do not wear any clothes and carry nothing with them except a soft broom made of shed peacock feathers (for sweeping bugs out of their path) and eat from their hands. They sleep on the floor without blankets, no matter how cold the weather may be and sit in the sun to meditate, no matter how hot.

Jain ascetics are strict vegetarians without root vegetables like carrots or beets. They don't cook any food and sometimes have only one meal per day, unless they are fasting. Fasting means they don't eat any food or drink any water for a period of time. Jain monk fasting can last from one day to a whole month.

> Do not love the world or the things in the world.
> If anyone loves the world, the love of the Father
> is not in him.
> ~1 John 2:15

Jainism defies a few boundaries that we have already set concerning what to look for when deciding which God we should choose. First, they have no god. For the most part, that should be the end of it. However, it does get interesting when you examine the Five Great Vows.

Mahavira was born the son of a minor ruler in northeast India. He married and had one daughter. Despite his position and wealth, he was not happy. At the age of thirty, after the death of his parents, Mahavira left his wife and child, turned his back on wealth and luxury and went off to join the ascetics in the pursuit of salvation.[27] Because he was from a family of wealthy rulers, it is probable that he had some schooling or education. He obviously, at some point (maybe then), came in contact with the Bible. He denied the Bible's claims that there is a God, but he clearly "borrowed" parts of both the Old and New Testaments and adopted them as his own.

The first three of his Five Great Vows come directly from the Ten Commandments that God gave Moses on Mount Sinai. These can be found in Exodus, chapter twenty, of the Bible. The fourth of the Five Great Vows is both an Old and New Testament teaching that condemns sexual immorality. The fifth vow came from teachings in the New Testament that he has taken out of context. He transformed these teachings into a type of torturous lifestyle rather than the instruction in a proper attitude towards the things of the world that have set themselves against God, as they were originally meant to be.

None of these teachings were known, taught, or practiced until they were first written down in the Bible. It's one thing to follow these biblical teachings, but if you are going to, it would be best to go back and follow the original teacher of them, rather than follow someone who sifts through and takes the things he can use, and distorts, changes, or omits the things he can't. It is said that imitation is the sincerest form of flattery, but taking the ideas of someone else and assuming credit for them is called plagiarism.

SIKHISM

Sikhism, which is centered in India, has about 27 million followers, but has only been around for approximately 500 years. Most followers, called Sikhs, live in India, although there are many dispersed around the world including approximately 1 million in the United States. Because of their appearance (their religion requires that men wear turbans and leave their beards uncut), Sikhs are often mistaken for Muslims and have been wrongly associated with Taliban. This had led to severely unfair treatment. There have been several incidents since September 11, 2001 in which Sikh members have been victims of hate crimes. In fact, since the 9/11 terrorist attacks, the Sikh Coalition, a New York-based advocacy group, reported more than 700 attacks or bias-related incidents against Sikhs.[28]

As recently as August, 2012, a neo-Nazi, white-supremacist, hate musician walked into and opened fire on a Sikh Temple in Milwaukee, Wisconsin. Apparently confusing them with Muslim terrorists, he killed six and critically wounded three others, including one police officer who was aiding a downed victim.[29]

In reality, the majority of Sikhs are peace-loving, gentle people. Attempts to maintain their pacifist roots are not always possible geographically, as in many areas of the world they find themselves in a crossfire between Muslims and Hindus, in part due to their founder Nanak's desire to harmonize the two.

Nanak (1469-1538) was born of a Hindu father and a Muslim mother in India. Because of his bold assertion, "There is no Muslim, and there is no Hindu," he accumulated a large number of followers. Guru Nanak developed a new religion that included what he thought were the good beliefs of these two religions.

Islam teaches the existence of one invisible god, while Hinduism believes in
Karma and reincarnation. Nanak figured out a way to make the two completely different ideas work together. He did this by changing the definition of enlightenment to mean a rebirth into a mystical union with god, rather than just an enlightened state of Nirvana with no god, as the Hindus believe. So he took the Hindu Nirvana, which is a transcendent state (an elevated existence beyond the life we experience now), in which there is neither suffering, desire, nor sense of self, and at which point you are released from the cycle of reincarnating life, and coupled it to a union with a god. He could now promise his Hindu followers that they could enjoy their enlightened state in the presence of a god, and his Muslim followers that they could enjoy the presence of their god while living in an enlightened state.

Nanak retained the doctrines of reincarnation and karma which are fundamental to many eastern religions in addition to Hinduism. These include Buddhism, Taoism, Jainism and others, primarily because there has to be some kind of motivation to work towards this enlightened goal.

Reincarnation is the belief that when you die, you come back as someone or something else. Karma is the belief that how you live in this life will determine what you are in the next life. These beliefs teach that this is an unending cycle equal to imprisonment, lasting until you live in such a way to cause your enlightenment or salvation.

Nanak was opposed to legalistic ritualism, such as in Jainism, also from India, and taught that one can escape the reincarnation cycle (Samsara) only through mystical union with God, which could be achieved through devotion and chanting. You may remember that Jainism believes this escape comes from keeping their Five Great Vows, which involve much suffering and self sacrifice and are not really attainable by average followers. Therefore, these followers would be doomed to return as something else in their next life based on how they lived in this one.[30]

The concept of Samsara is closely associated with the belief that one continues to be born and reborn in various realms in the form of a human, animal, or other being (depending on karma). In particular, Jainism maintains that if one performs extremely evil karma, they will come back as a plant or even as a rock. Coming back as a rock, I guess, would mean that you would be a rock throughout eternity, since you would not have the opportunity to die and recycle.[31]

Sikhs, then, obviously believe, like Hindus, in the cycle of life. This would mean life, death, and then rebirth (life again). Relief from this cycle into unity with god can only be obtained with the help of a guru. This is where it gets a little difficult, because Sikhs no longer have a live guru. Gobind Singh, who was assassinated by Muslims in 1708, was the last human Sikh guru. The Sikh holy book, the Adi Granth, also called Guru Granth, took his place. The Adi Granth, while not worshipped, is considered by Sikhs to be divine. Singh affirmed that the Adi Granth was to be his successor.

To their credit, as mentioned, Sikhism teaches the existence of one god, Ik Onkar. Nanak taught that the creator and creation are inseparable, in the way that an ocean is made up of its individual drops.

Unlike Jainism founder Mahavira, who taught salvation by self-denial through a torturous lifestyle, Nanak's message can be briefly summarized as a doctrine of salvation through disciplined meditation on the divine name. The divine name signifies the total manifestation of god, a single being, immanent both in the created world and within the human spirit. Meditation must be strictly inward, and all external aids such as idols, temples, mosques, scriptures, and set prayers are explicitly rejected. This would not come naturally, as simply talking with God does, but would have to come from being educated into this system. While the Muslim influence is relatively slight, the influence of Hindu mystical and devotional beliefs is much more prevalent.

The whole idea of the existence of one God, immanent both in the created world and within the human spirit, comes ever so close to the biblical teaching that God is One, He is everywhere present (immanent in the created world) and He sends His Spirit to dwell with believers.

It seems fairly certain that Nanak was originally trying to find a way to bring peace to the two sides of his family. He must have seen some horrific family gatherings in his early years. There was an overwhelming acceptance of his ideas from the start, probably due in part to the similar longing of many other people for a unifying peace, and now they wouldn't have to suffer through severe self-sacrifice to gain salvation.

BUDDHISM

> To force oneself to believe and to accept a thing without understanding is political, and not spiritual or intellectual.
> ~Siddhartha Gautama (Buddha)

There could be as many as 500 million followers of Buddha. Buddha did not claim to be a god, and also did not believe in a god, so that right there should be reason enough to pass on this one. Then why is it so popular?

The main reasons that Buddhism may be a consideration for someone seeking a god to follow are one, it is the fourth largest religion in the world today, two, it has been around for 2,500 years and three, although it is primarily an eastern religion, it has lately become much more popular in the western world. Buddhism has answers to many of the problems in modern materialistic societies and boasts a deep understanding of the human mind.

Buddhists utilize natural therapies, which modern psychologists around the world are now discovering to be both very advanced and effective, but honestly, you can Google most of these things and practice them on your own without becoming a Buddhist, so this seems more like going back to worshiping the things God created rather than the God who created them.

Buddhism's founder, Siddhartha Guatama, was born into royalty in India around 600 BC. After four meaningful dreams, he decided to abandon his wealthy lifestyle and pursue enlightenment through a life of rigorous self-denial, or austerity, called asceticism. His efforts did not go unrewarded, as he became the "first" person to achieve enlightenment, and became known as the "enlightened one" or the "Buddha."

Buddhism, though, is clearly more of a way of life (this life) than a way to prepare for the next life, which, anyone who is truly seeking God probably understands to be heaven, or at least a heaven-like place.

Its teachings have much in common with many of the other eastern religions such as karma, reincarnation, and Maya (the belief that the material world and even life itself is an illusion).

Also, even though there was one original Buddha (Siddhartha Guatama) and his teachings, there are now at least two divisions of Buddhism with many branches or subdivisions such as Tendai, Vajrayana, Nichiren, Shingon, Pure Land, Zen and Ryobu, among others. Therefore, beyond these three general teachings, it's hard to know what any one school of Buddhism believes without studying each one individually.[32] Buddhists have to go through a lot of suffering, self sacrifice, and right living as defined in their doctrines in order to reach enlightenment during their lifetime. Whether they reach it or not, because they're Buddhists, they probably don't believe in God. The real God would likely take offense to that. I would. There is strong evidence that He will not take kindly to any of those who do not believe in Him.

HINDUISM

> What Brahman is cannot be described. All things in the world—the Vedas, the Puranas, the Tantras, the six systems of philosophy—have been defiled, like food that has been touched by the tongue, for they have been read or uttered by the tongue. Only one thing has not been defiled in this way, and that is Brahman. No one has ever been able to say what Brahman is.
> ~Ramakrishna, Sayings of Sri Ramakrishna
> (1836-1886)

Hinduism is the last near-eastern religion that we will look at. Hinduism is enormous; with nearly a billion followers, it represents 15 percent of the world's population. Trying to understand Hinduism can give you a headache. It is extremely diversified in its beliefs and can have as many as 330 million gods, but at the same time one god named Brahma who is supreme over all other gods.

Brahma is an entity believed to inhabit every portion of reality and existence throughout the entire universe. Brahma is both impersonal and unknowable and is often believed to exist in three separate forms: Brahma (creator), Vishnu (preserver), and Shiva (destroyer).

Hinduism is one of the oldest known organized religions. Its sacred writings possibly date as far back as 1400 BC, which would be just after the time of Moses. Hindus have a wide variety of core beliefs and exist in many different sects. Although it is the third largest religion in the world, Hinduism exists primarily in India and Nepal.[33]

As far as their theology (what they believe about God), the various Hindu schools contain elements of almost every theological system. However, Hindus do have a group of written texts on which they base their beliefs. The main text is the Vedas. The litmus test for Hinduism seems to be whether or not a belief system recognizes the Vedas as sacred. If it does, then it is Hindu. If it doesn't, it has no part in Hinduism.

The goal seems to be to find a way to become one with Brahma. Until you can do this, you are only living a life of illusion. By becoming one with Brahma, you are freed from this illusory state. This freedom is known to the Hindu as moksha. To know how to reach this goal, you would have to find out what the beliefs are of the Hindu branch you join. And, according to Hindu teaching, until you achieve it, you are doomed to be repeatedly reincarnated into a next life each time you die. What you become in the next life depends on how you live this life, which again, is called karma.

Many years ago, my wife's aunt from New York City came for a brief visit. We took her out to a quaint little Italian restaurant that had surprisingly good food. While we were eating, I swatted at a fly that was buzzing around me. My wife's aunt freaked out and started yelling at me not to kill the fly. This woman was easily in her forties, maybe even fifties, but she was convinced that I might be trying to kill her father. Needless to say, I didn't move for a second, wondering if I might have just entered the Twilight Zone.

I'm not sure if her father was kidding around with her (as fathers do) and forgot to tell her, or just never got the chance, but he had convinced her that when he died he would be coming back as a fly. She was still young when he met an untimely death (by being struck in the head by a beer bottle during a barroom brawl, as I recall), and he went to his grave, leaving her to believe that he would come back and be found flying around her food.

AS HARD AS IT IS TO BELIEVE THAT AN ADULT COULD THINK THIS WAY, IT IS A CORE BELIEF OF A BILLION PEOPLE.

There is no one single person that the origin of this religion can be attributed to, with the exception that it appears that Brahma, the main god of Hinduism, was the creator in early Hindu mythology, and literally thousands of sages have contributed to the Hindu belief system that sprang from this myth according to their individual philosophies.

THE SOUTHEAST END

If you read through these Southeast Asian religions carefully, you've probably noticed a pattern that weaves between each of them. Even though they are taking different paths, they are all trying to find their way from here to somewhere else. It is the goal of all of these religions that believe in reincarnation and karma to somehow escape this process. That's what they're trying to do with all the chanting, yoga, self denial, meditation, and suffering.

Where this idea of reincarnation ever came from in the first place, I do not know, and it is doubtful that anyone does for sure. It is reported by archeologists that the early Egyptians wanted to have themselves mummified because they believed they would need to have their body preserved in order to come back in another life. If mummified properly, their bodies would be recognizable to their souls, which had left their bodies when they died, but would return to be reunited with it and live forever. That is a stretch, I know, but, since 1967, nearly 200 people have had their bodies frozen through a process called cryonics and stored for the future in hopes of someday being thawed out and brought back to life. The process to preserve a whole body now costs around $200,000, but it does cost less (around $80,000) for just a head or other partial body section if you can't afford the whole shot. There are at least four companies available to provide this service for you.

Ironically, Hindu reincarnation theories, among the earliest known, which began after the Egyptian's mummification theories were devised, incorporate cremation of a person's remains. If these ideas branched out from one original place, it would make sense that whoever came up with the Hindu idea for sure didn't want any chance of his soul finding its way back to the same body. They must have figured incineration was the best bet.

As far as this section of the world goes, if you started in the Turkey/Iraq vicinity (which historical books as well archeological evidence pinpoint as the area of the earliest human civilization), and went in different directions, you couldn't get much farther apart than from Egypt to India, just as you definitely can't get much farther apart than from mummification to cremation.

Chapter Eight

FROM MOONIES TO MORMONS

OTHER CULTS AND RELIGIONS THAT HAVE SPRUNG FROM THE BIBLE

During the 1970s the Unification Church became very popular, especially among the hippie movement and young people looking for alternative religions. You may have heard of them referred to as "Moonies." If you are a young person reading this book, you may have at least been a little curious about their teachings of peace and love and their apparent carefree lifestyle. Their original leader, the late Sun Myung Moon, taught that he was the messiah and had been crowned the king of Christianity. He believed that he was the second coming of Christ and had come to fulfill what Jesus did not do.

In recent years, however, membership has dwindled drastically due in part to Moon's conviction of tax fraud against the United States. There have been multiple reports of the Moon family's dysfunction, including spousal abuse and drug addiction by Moon's oldest son, suicide by another son, and children fathered by Sun Myung Moon's adulterous relationships with followers. Add to this the fact that the Moons live in glorious mansions around the world while Unification Church members sell flowers on street corners and are servants to obnoxious family members, and you can see why being a Moonie has become less attractive.

However, at Rev. Moon's burial ceremony at a church-owned facility that is fashioned after the White House, 35,000 mourners made the trek to Gapyeong, South Korea to pay their final respects.

After a recent highly publicized mass wedding on television, Steve Hassan, an ex-Unification Church leader, voiced his concerns by lamenting, "I feel bad for the couples on the show. I wish I could sit down and talk with them and let them know I was one of Father's chosen leaders and that the teachings of the group need to be examined before they even think of having children as this is not a healthy organization," as he spoke with RadarOnline.com in an exclusive interview.[34]

Mass weddings in the Unification Church many times involve church members who are joined together in arranged marriages. The women and consequent children legally belong to the church leadership. So, if the husband tries to leave the organization once he realizes he's been lied to and used in order to keep his leaders living in luxury, he must leave his wife and children behind. (Arranging for people to marry who come from different countries also helps the Unification Church to get around immigration laws when they need to move servants from country to country.)

Unfortunately, this cult may once again begin growing rapidly. Since Moon's death on September 3, 2012, his son, Hyung Jin Moon, and Rev. Moon's widow who succeeds her husband as head of the church, have been planning vast, worldwide expansion.

Hyung Jin Moon, speaking at his father's funeral

ceremony, discussed at length plans to carry on the work of his father's last great project for a global "Nation of Cosmic Peace and Unity." They had a "Foundation Day" planned for this new movement which was set for January 13, 2013.

Recently, under the direction of the late Rev. Sun Myung Moon, known by unificationists as Father Moon or True Father, unificationist ministers made it a goal to reach out to 13,000 faith leaders by February 22, 2013. Through the blindly dedicated efforts of unificationists, a total of 8,000 faith leaders have already been educated—62 percent of Father Moon's pronounced goal before he passed away September 3, 2012. For the first time, the Unificationist commentary on the Bible, known as the Original Substance of the Divine Principle (OSDP), has been broadcast nationwide, and thousands of American clergy have participated.[35]

It seems unbelievable that anybody could be lured into this trap, considering all the information that is available to expose its wrongdoings, but it is well baited. If you are truly looking for the right God to follow, it shouldn't be one that has been divorced twice, abandoned a wife and son, launders money, bribes politicians, or is involved in extortion. These are attributes that you would expect to be associated with a corrupt, money hungry manipulator, but certainly not the true God, or according to Rev. Moon's self-proclamation, His Son.

Even though this cult has taken many ideas from the Bible, it has transformed these ideas to fit their own itinerary and form a highly successful financial empire which is built entirely on lies. To take anything from the Bible and change it is fraud at best and to manipulate innocent, unsuspecting young people with these blatant lies is heinous.

This is a highly deceptive and enticing cult with an open door for those who are weary from battling the ruthless tactics of society and are looking for a quick, simple solution. Their websites and literature promise peace and unity, but good advice here would be to determine ahead of time, at what cost?

THE MORMON CHURCH AKA THE CHURCH OF LATTER DAY SAINTS

There are approximately 14 million Mormons in the world today. This is troubling when you realize that this is yet another cult that has spun off from the Bible. That alone is reason enough to scratch this one off your list. Mormons use parts of the Bible along with three other books as a basis for their beliefs. Of the four books they use, (The Book of Mormon, Doctrine and Covenants, Pearl of Great Price, and parts of the Bible), the Bible is the only one they consider *not* to be infallible, or without error.

Among some of the scarier things that Mormons believe are that "God was a man on another planet,"[36] "(God) the father has a body of flesh and bones as tangible as man's,"[37] "God himself was once as we are now, and is an exalted man, and sits enthroned in yonder heavens!" Their prophet Joseph Smith wrote, "We have imagined that God was God from all eternity. I will refute that idea and take away the veil, so that you may see,"[38] "After you become a good Mormon, you have the potential of becoming a god,"[39] (*this is why they are referred to as the "god makers"*), "There is a mother god"[40] and "God is married to his goddess wife and has spirit children."[41]

Plus, Mormons believe that Satan is the literal son of God and the brother of Jesus Christ, and, at least among the worst of all, they also believe that their own three books are the infallible Word of God.

I have to refer back to a point made earlier which stated that when the Bible was completed nearly 2,000 years ago, it was accepted as the infallible Word of God, and meets all of the criteria for accepted historical truth. The Apostle Paul made it clear when he wrote about his concerns for the church in Corinth, "But I am afraid that your minds will be led away from your true and pure following of Christ just as Eve was tricked by the snake with his evil ways. You are very patient with anyone who comes to you and preaches a different Jesus from the one we preached. You are very willing to accept a spirit or gospel that is different from the Spirit and Good News you received from us" (2 Corinthians 11:3-4).

It is clear that the spirit and gospel that followers receive from The Book of Mormon, Doctrine and Covenants and The Pearl of Great Price is different from the Spirit and Good News that followers received from the Apostle Paul and the other Bible writers.

The Bible says that God's Word is settled forever in Heaven. It stands to reason, then, that there cannot be another Word of God, just like there cannot be another God, and if there were any extension of the Word of God (which there is not) it would be perfect and infallible just as the original, because God cannot contradict Himself. Contradiction is not one of the attributes of God, just like lying isn't. Incidentally, the Bible also states that Jesus *is* the Word of God. The Mormons do not believe any of the claims of or about Christ that are recorded in the Bible. It probably goes without saying that there are many, many disparities between the Bible and the books of Mormon. If you truly want to follow the right God, then you would have to choose between these two, because they both don't agree.

Which God Should I Choose?

Up to the time of Joseph Smith, who wrote the Book of Mormon in 1830, it had been over 1,800 years since the early church leaders agreed that the Word of God was complete. They understood that all scripture was inspired by God to its writers, who are called holy men of God. God did not send angels to give messages to men to write down once the Bible was completed. God breathed His Word directly to these men. Early church leaders met and compiled for us what is today known as the Canon of Scripture.

You may have heard the term Canon of Scripture before and wondered exactly what that meant. Simply stated, the Canon of Scripture is the group of historical books accepted by both the ancient Israelites (Old Testament) and the early Christian church leaders (both Old and New Testament) as the inspired Word of God. It is what we call the Holy Bible today.

The earliest known acceptance of the books of the Bible as we know them dates from before 400 BC for the Old Testament and from 100 AD for the New Testament.

As for the Israelites, in spite of some other writings appearing in the third century BC Greek translation called the Septuagint, only the books that had been accepted as Holy Scripture prior to the fourth century BC were accepted as part of the Jewish canon. Although they are in a different order, we have these same identical books today in what we call the Old Testament of the Bible.

As for the New Testament, towards the end of the first century, the books and letters that had been written by the apostles, their close companions Luke and Mark, and the brothers of Jesus, James and Jude, were collected and packaged for circulation to Christian churches. The Apostle John, who lived to the end of the first century, may have played a part in that endeavor.

Beginning around 100 AD, several early church leaders, including the Apostle John's companion Polycarp, mentioned many of these books by name in their own writings. The first known New Testament Canon was called the Muratorian Canon. It was compiled in 170 AD and included all of the New Testament books except the book called Hebrews.

By 363 AD, at the council of Laodicea, it was affirmed that all of the Old and New Testament books (including Hebrews), exactly as we have them today, should be accepted as the complete, inspired Word of God.

And so, I mention all of this because it took little time for men who had devoted their lives in service to God to assemble and decide upon what should be accepted as God's Word to man. They had certain criteria that they followed in the process.

For the Old Testament, early Christian church leaders, who were at the beginning mostly Jewish, used exactly what the Israelites considered to be their Holy Scriptures. The prophet Ezra assembled these books that were considered to be the Canon of Scripture. Included in this Canon were the writings of Ezra, as well as Nehemiah and Malachi who were his contemporaries and, as far as we know, were the last prophets that God spoke to before Christ. Anything written later than Ezra, Nehemiah, and Malachi is excluded from the Jewish Canon because it was understood that God had stopped speaking to prophets around 400 BC, and remained silent for the next 400 years.

That is why you do not see the collection of books called the Apocrypha included in accepted Protestant Bibles. These books were written during a time when God was silent as far as communicating His Word to man (from 400 BC until the birth of Christ), and so are not believed to be inspired by God, which is the definition of true Scripture. Ezra surely would have been aware of any Egyptian writings on gold plates[42] that were inspired by God, because they first would have been written in Hebrew and handed down both orally and in scroll form to all generations, and he would have included them in his compilation of Scripture.

Hebrews 1:1 says, "In the past God spoke to our ancestors through the prophets many times and in many different ways." 2 Timothy 3:16 tells us, "All Scripture is *inspired* by God and is useful for teaching, for showing people what is wrong in their lives, for correcting faults, and for teaching how to live right." The word translated "inspired" here is the Greek word *theopneustos*, which means "God-breathed." At this point in time, the Apostle Paul was speaking of what we call the Old Testament because the New Testament had not yet been completed.

The criteria used for determining what could be included in New Testament Canon were pretty simple. A book or letter had to be verified that it was written by an apostle of God, by one of their companions who were under their authority, or by a companion of Jesus Himself. There are a lot of early books not included in the New Testament because, at the time they were composed, they were known *not* to have been written by one of these men. In other words, they were known to be forgeries. Many of these books are still available today, and some are even called "lost" books of the Bible, but they were not lost at all. They were not included because they were not inspired by God. They did not meet the criteria then by the standards of the Christian leaders who were alive when they were written, so, they should definitely not be thought of as Scripture today, and should be avoided if at all possible.

Together, the Old Testament Hebrew Canon coupled

with the New Testament early church Canon is today known as the Holy Bible. It seems odd that anyone would think that this original, complete written Word of God would need to be amended, and by an unknown angel at that. Yet the Mormons hold that new additional scriptures were given by an angel to their original leader, Joseph Smith. As you study the Bible you will realize that it covers every facet of human existence. It is the complete handbook for living a godly life. Anything else that is written in addition to what is in the Bible would have to disagree with it, because there's nothing that needs to be added. And, there can only be one truth. On the other hand, there can be many lies.

That brings us back to the Book of Mormon. It does not meet any criteria at all for being considered as coming from God, and if carefully examined, it becomes obvious that it is a not-so-clever forgery. It was supposedly translated by Joseph Smith from ancient gold plates but actually quotes the King James Bible word for word throughout the book, including several translation errors. As you think about that, if you were to translate ancient Egyptian writings from 2,000 to 3,000 years ago into 1830s American English, would it come out word for word with the King James Bible, which was translated from Greek into King James's 1600s English? Obviously not. No Christians were fooled at the time, and Joseph Smith was considered a heretic. So, as with every other cult or religion that has taken the Bible and changed it to meet their own purposes, a new cult had to be formed.

Mormons must memorize thirteen articles, or fundamentals, of Mormon belief. There are so many discrepancies between Biblical truth and these articles that I would hardly know where to start if it were not for the fact that in general, Mormons do not believe in grace, which according to Ephesians 2:8-9, is the only way a person can be saved.

Even among individual Mormons there are many varying beliefs. In other words, they do not all believe the same thing. I always refer to this as a moving line. In my mind, it's impossible to take a stand when the line you must cross is moving back and forth.

In 1836, Lieutenant Colonel William Travis drew a line in the sand with his sword. He and his men, numbering less than two hundred, were completely surrounded by upwards of 4,000 enemy soldiers. They were defending a little fortified mission called the Alamo. They had held out for twelve days while President General Antonio Lopez de Santa Anna gathered his huge army together in preparation for a final assault. Lieutenant Colonel Travis told his men that although he had dispatched several letters asking for help, no reinforcements would come. By drawing that line in the sand, he was asking his men to take a stand. Anyone who wanted to leave, could leave. If they chose to stay, they must cross that line and join him. All but one crossed over the line to stand with Lieutenant Colonel Travis. They understood the consequences because Lieutenant Colonel Travis had told them the truth. Anyone who decided to stay would die in their defense of freedom. The Mexican army did not take prisoners.

It's so important to have a line that does not move. The truth can never move. It can never change. The truth cannot be found in discrepancies. If three people say three different things, at least two, and maybe all three, are wrong.

Millions of unsuspecting people have accepted the Mormon god as truth. I would have to suppose that they made this decision without ever considering the facts. There is not a shred of truth in the Mormon doctrine.

They use the Bible as a smokescreen to lure in unsuspecting converts, but believe the Bible to be filled with errors and distort its truth.

If you are a part of this organization already or have been considering it as a possible choice, I encourage you to research the evidence that I have gathered here so that you can be sure that, in your quest to find the right God, the Mormon god is not the god who is right for you. You can trust the evidence. He is not the god you should choose.

Chapter Nine

THE OPRAH CHURCH

This is kind of a New Age religion with a twist. Basically, I guess, you become your own god. It's interesting that, although Oprah says she first rejected what the Bible presents to us because "it didn't feel right," most of their beliefs evolve from Bible terms. Oprah repeatedly contradicts God's Word. She continues to reject the "negatives" of biblical faith, such as man being a fallen sinner and needing redemption through Christ's death at Calvary, but she tries to hold on to the more "positive" aspects of love, hope, peace, grace, and blessing.

One of the Oprah church's teachers is author and lecturer Eckhart Tolle. Oprah and Tolle state that orthodox Christians have merely manufactured a "god" in their own image—that he is a product of their warped imagination. Oprah's weekly online seminar, based on Eckhart Tolle's book, *The New Earth*, is called "walking you through a new birth," which is another "borrowed" biblical term. In the Bible, Jesus uses the phrase "you must be born again" to explain how a person will be able to enter God's Kingdom. Even more interesting is that this statement by Jesus actually refutes the theory of evolution, which Oprah apparently believes. She is quoted as saying, "The whole point of being alive is to evolve into the complete person you were intended to be."

Gary Zukav, another Oprah church teacher, says, "Souls that have chosen the physical experience of life as we know it as a path of evolution, have, in general, incarnated their energies many times into many psychological and physical forms. For each incarnation, the *soul* creates a different personality and body." Sounds like yet another twist on the biblical term, being "born again." Also sounds a little like a dose of Hinduism mixed with a back-door version of what is called pantheism—God is in everything and everything is God.

Oprah church leaders say God is not "up there." He (or it) is in every person; we have only to seek the divine consciousness or force within. As Oprah remarked to Tolle, "God is a feeling experience, not a believing experience—otherwise it's not truly God." She said, "We are the universe, or the source of all life, the creator, or god."[43]

I recently heard an atheist evolutionist say that your brain is who you are; it tells you what to do. "When your brain, dies it rots. When your brain dies, you die." That what evolution says. We come from nothing and return to nothing.

On the other hand, when Jesus said, "You must be born again," He was explaining how a person can enter God's Kingdom. When you turn to Him in faith, you become a child of God, and heaven becomes your eternal home. When your body dies, you actually pass from physical death in this life to spiritual life with Jesus instantly. There is no evolving or reincarnating experience at all. If you haven't been *born again*, you pass from physical death in this life directly to spiritual death in hell.

When you are born again according to Jesus, you

actually become a new creation with a whole new, completely different set of values and belief system. If you hated before, now you love; if you were dissatisfied before, now you are content; if you were miserable before, now you have joy; if you had unrest before, now you have peace. It's 100 percent different—a complete turn around. Your brain was in control before and you were at the mercy of your feelings. But now, God's Spirit is in control and helps your spirit control your thoughts.

If the evolutionist is correct and the brain is in control (that it's who we are and tells us what to do), then it would also have to be able to change its way of thinking and tell you to become someone else completely different and be able to do that at a moment's notice, because that's exactly what happens when a person turns their heart (who they really are) to Jesus. If this were a rare occurrence, then you might be able to say it's possible for the brain to malfunction like this in isolated incidents, but the fact is that this transformation takes place for every single person who gives their life to Christ and has for the past 1,979 years, thousands and perhaps millions of times over. Remember, our brains lean toward what is wrong and since Jesus is the enemy of evolution, it is highly unlikely that a brain that knows it's going to rot when it dies would turn to Jesus.

Even if you yourself have never made this decision or experienced this transformation, I encourage you to seek out some people who say they have given their life to Christ and have been "born again." Question as many of them as you can find. You will be amazed to see how similar each testimony of what God has done in their lives will be.

Eckhart Tolle also misrepresents what it means for believers to serve as lights in the world. He quotes Jesus' words, "You are the light of the world," adding that this means, "You are the consciousness in which the world appears—is seen." Whatever that means.

And what about the Oprah church's concept of heaven? Tolle says, "Heaven is not a location, but refers to the inner realm of consciousness." It is important for us to know that heaven was created by God in the first place, and its story was written down in the Bible long before anyone tried to move its location or redesign its features.

The Oprah church is centered more around self than a true spiritual encounter with God and focuses on the betterment of our psychological beings—with a large dose of material prosperity thrown in. But it is devoid of true spiritual life. Oprah defines spirituality as "being reminded about the best part of who you are." Positive-thinking spirituality is nothing new. It's been around since the beginning and has led millions of people down the wrong path. This particular brand is in a fresh new package aimed more toward females than males, so ladies, be careful. If you are truly seeking the right God to follow, please do not allow yourself to be drawn into this trap. Simplifying your life and developing positive-thinking can make life here on earth seem more fulfilling, but at the end of the day, we will still have to face God.

The Oprah Church promises "meaning without truth, acceptance without judgment, and fulfillment without self-denial." Oprah states, "I am a Christian who believes there are certainly many more paths to God other than Christianity. ... It's a mistake to believe that there's only one way. There are millions of ways to what you call 'God.'"

Oprah's book, *Live Your Best Life*, written in 2005, describes her philosophy that everything is one and man is divine and can create his own reality. Her gospel is that man is not a sinner, God is not a judge, all is well with the universe, and I just need to surrender to the flow. She encourages people to meditate and pray. She says that it doesn't matter to what you pray—to God or to Glorious Future or to all that is Divine or to all that is Love, or whatever.[43]

Remember how at the beginning of this book we looked at the error in believing that the same person who messed up our life in the first place has the hidden power to make things right again?

There is absolutely no truth in any of this teaching. It is based on a foundation of emotion and confusion. These are not the indicators that should be steering us toward the right God.

Remember, to start a new religion from scratch is bad enough, but to take an already established religion, change its doctrine, and then call it your own is always found in deceptive practices used by forgers for personal gain—whether it be power, fame, or fortune.

UNITARIAN UNIVERSALISM – SECULAR HUMANISM – POST MODERNISM

Talk about a lot of fancy ways to say the same thing. These groups or cults all have different titles but pretty much share the same belief system, and eventually all lead to the same outcome. They cater to the free thinkers of today's society that believe they can control their own destiny according to what they believe.

These are the feel-good, do your own thing, and be your own god religions that give people from all sorts of belief systems the opportunity to fit in together, without judgment. They share thoughts between many religions, including the eastern religions that teach inner peace and spiritual maturity through self-redemption.

In these systems you are the boss of your own life and you can basically build your own religion like a make-your-own sundae. You can design it by what you personally believe to be true. This fits nicely with the stubborn, prideful, arrogant attitude of those that would rather find a way to make themselves spiritually fulfilled rather than believe that there is a real God and trust in Him for their salvation.

They believe that mankind is inherently good and able to redeem themselves without the need for any assistance from God. There is no absolute truth, so you can believe whatever you want to. Whatever seems right to you is where you can set your standards.

Unitarian Universalism has no set beliefs, and that is its defining characteristic. They state, "We believe that personal experience, conscience, and reason should be the final authorities in religion, and that in the end religious authority lies not in a book or person or institution, but in ourselves. We are a 'non-creedal' religion: we do not ask anyone to subscribe to a creed." It goes without saying that there are a lot of different beliefs within these organizations, and their church meetings look more like a country club than a worship service. Some of the belief groups that gather together under the umbrella of Unitarian Universalism are secular humanist, agnostic, earth-centered, atheist, Buddhist, pagan, and Christian (in name only). This great diversity within one congregation is perhaps eased by the fact that Unitarian Universalism tends to emphasize the importance of action over belief.[44]

These groups teach, among other things, that you should be able to decide what is right for you. Morality is based on the standards you set for yourself, so you are not accountable to anybody, especially God, for your actions. If it feels good, do it. If you want to be an atheist, that is fine. If you want to believe in a god, you can believe in the god you want and worship him however you want.

Since there are no rules, it is easy for everyone involved to stray from an absolute standard of truth and use the moving line theory that truth moves depending on the situation and is relative to experience. That makes it a lot easier to deny the need for, the power of, or the existence of God.

You would definitely do well to steer clear of any religion or belief system like this that promises a way to spiritual enlightenment or salvation by taking control of your own fate or destiny and becoming the god of your own life. Since there is a real God who is opposed to this kind of thinking, there can be no future in this, either in this life or the life to come. As you look back through history, you will find that there was no pot of gold at the end of the rainbow for anyone who ever fell for this kind of self-righteous religion.

SCIENTOLOGY

I'd like to start a religion—that's where the money is.
~L. Ron Hubbard (1911-1986)

Because Scientology categorically denies the existence of the God, this cult is probably not going to be a good fit for anyone who is seeking to find the right God. In fact, unless you are very wealthy, Scientology will not fit into your budget either, as it costs hundreds of thousands of dollars to reach salvation through this method, and then, as we will discover, this salvation is not salvation at all, but just another avenue that leads to self-righteousness for the follower and great wealth for the leader. Every aspect of Scientology has some sort of fee associated with it. It is a strict and private cult that has heavily guarded communes with armed security guards, razor-wire fences, motion detectors, and infrared sensors that makes it very difficult to leave once you have become a part of it. An ABC News report states that members are not allowed to leave the properties without permission, and if they do go AWOL, they are tracked down by military-style teams who are allowed to inflict emotional or physical punishment. Children are distanced from their parents and go through a series of brainwashing-type procedures as a replacement to education. Those who leave successfully are often burdened with feelings of guilt that have been ingrained into their consciences.

Scientology's "scriptures" are limited solely to the writings and teachings of deceased founder L. Ron Hubbard. He founded Scientology in 1953, just four years after making the public statement, "I'd like to start a religion—that's where the money is."

Scientology's bizarre teachings come straight from the science fiction stories devised by their founder. Some teachings include that mankind is an immortal being (called a Thetan) from another planet who is trapped by matter, energy, space, and time (MEST). Salvation for a Scientologist comes through a process called "auditing," whereby "engrams" (basically, memories of past pain and unconsciousness that create energy blockage) are removed. Auditing is a lengthy process and can cost hundreds of thousands of dollars. When all engrams are finally removed, the Thetan can once again control MEST instead of being controlled by it. Until salvation, each Thetan is constantly reincarnated. (This is why they take children away from their parents and start "teaching" them at a young age, because very few intelligent adults are going to fall for this nonsense.) So, like many Eastern religions, Scientology also believes in reincarnation and that personal salvation in one's lifetime is freedom from the cycle of birth and death associated with reincarnation.[46]

Scientology also holds to the unrealistic belief that there is inherent goodness in man, and teaches that it is despicable and utterly beneath contempt to tell a man he must repent or that he is evil. To emphasize just how ridiculous this philosophy is, imagine turning loose the millions of felons that are in the world's prisons today and telling them, "It's okay; you're not really bad and you don't have to pay for what you did."

After reading about the dangers of cults, especially ones that use military compounds, guards, and brainwashing techniques, you will have to agree that it sounds like this organization is cooking with a recipe for disaster. It seems like it can only be just a matter of time before someone triggers the switch that leads to tragedy for this prison-style money trap.

You may be reading this book and right now are somehow involved with this cult, or one like it. I encourage you to set yourself free ASAP—somehow, someway, whatever it takes. It's a dead end, whether you quit now and start heading in the right direction or wait until later. The problem with waiting until later is that the longer you wait, the harder getting out will be and the more time you will have wasted.

Chapter Ten

THE GOD OF THIS WORLD

At the end of a *successful* search, you will find that there is only One God and that you have found and chosen the right One. However, just as there is only one real God, there is really, at the heart of it all, only one false god as well. So, the choice invariably reverts back to right or wrong, black or white, one or the other. I know throughout this book I have touched on one false god after another, but the simple truth is that all false gods that there have ever been or will ever be default back to one source. He is the god of this world who has been around since the beginning and is the ultimate deceiver. He is the chief enemy of the real God. His given name is Lucifer, but you may know him by other names such as Satan or the devil. He really does have a master plan, and if God did not have total control over the entire situation, it would be far more successful.

Satan uses many strategies to gain followers and confuse the world's population. In relation to false gods, his plan is simple, yet effective.

Say someone owns a company that makes an ineffective laundry detergent and decides to buy up all their competitors' brands (even though they don't work either) so that everybody has to buy their detergent from them. It doesn't matter how many different brands of laundry detergent there are, because they will own them all: actually, the more the merrier. The more there are, the more choices people have. They love the variety of products and the apparent competitiveness between them. Seldom does anyone ever realize that none of these detergents work.

At the same time, there is still one company that is separate from this monopoly that has, ironically, the only detergent that really works. The workers who make all of the other detergent brands for the ineffective company hate the good detergent Maker and lie about Him, put down His product, and make fun of His workers. In many countries they actually try to kill this one good company's workers.

Similarly, it really doesn't matter to Satan how many false gods there are because, ultimately, all of the profit from all of the products goes to him—the spiritual profit, that is. It is true that he is not, at least on the surface, getting the glory from the worship of all these false gods, but, for every single person that he can get to follow one of his products, that is one more person that he has successfully led away from the one true God.

There is a real battle going on out there for each soul in the world. It is a spiritual battle and not one like the wars that we are used to, where people fight to kill flesh and blood. It is spiritual because your heart—your innermost being, the part of you that thinks and plans, the part of you that tells your brain what to do—is the prize. Although someday we will receive a new body from God, our spirit, right now, is the part of us that is eternal.

In John 14, Jesus referred to Satan as the ruler of this world, but went on to point out that Satan had no power over Him. The Apostle Paul, in 2 Corinthians 4:4, also calls him the ruler of this world and many times this is actually translated the god of this world. Paul goes on to say he "has blinded the minds of those who do not believe. They cannot see the light of the Good News—the Good News about the glory of Christ, who is exactly like God."

Clearly, one of the ways he blinds the eyes of those who do not believe is by his tactics of confusion.

WHERE DID HE COME FROM?

Early on, in Genesis chapter three, we first hear of Satan. He is only referred to here as the "clever snake" and is not really named. Older translations call him the subtle or cunning serpent. But later, in Revelation 12:9, John clears this up. He writes, "The giant dragon was thrown down out of heaven. (He is that old snake called the devil or Satan, who tricks the whole world.) The dragon with his angels was thrown down to the earth." And in Revelation 20:22, he says, "The angel grabbed the dragon, that old snake who is the devil and Satan, and tied him up for a thousand years." Unfortunately, he was more clever than either Adam or Eve and fooled them both into rebelling against God, which inevitably led to the fall of man.

The "fall of man" is a term used for this incident in ancient history, although not a term found in the Bible. Up until that day, Adam and Eve lived in innocence with God, in a perfect paradise called Eden. In Eden there was no sin or death. All inhabitants were vegetarians, so they did not have a desire to eat one another. God instructed Adam and Eve to eat from any tree in the garden they wanted, but "you must not eat the fruit from the tree which gives the knowledge of good and evil" (Genesis 2:17). Subsequently, Satan talked them into doing just that—eating the only fruit that was forbidden for them to eat. This fruit carried a deadly, transmittable disease called sin. Once infected, there was no known cure. So, by rebelling against God in this manner, what is known as the "sin nature" entered their systems. In consequence of this, being the parents of all mankind, their newfound sin nature was transmitted to every descendent that has lived since them.

This is where we first hear of Satan. God, on the other hand, had known a bit about him prior to this event. God had created him as one of His most beautiful creations. Satan was referred to in Isaiah as the morning star and was as bright in appearance as the rising sun (Isaiah 14). Ezekiel tells us, "This is what the Lord God says: You were an example of what was perfect, full of wisdom and perfect in beauty." He goes on to say, "Every valuable gem was on you: ruby, topaz, and emerald, yellow quartz, onyx, and jasper, sapphire, turquoise, and chrysolite. Your jewelry was made of gold. It was prepared on the day you were created" (Ezekiel 28:2-14).

Satan became filled with pride though, because of his beauty, and said to himself, "I will put my throne above God's stars. I will go up above the tops of the clouds. I will be like God Most High" (Isaiah 14:13-14).

Well, that didn't work, and on that account, he was cast out of Heaven by God. He has pretty much been banished from heaven ever since, although he apparently has to check in now and then, as we see in Job chapters one and two. In both chapters we see the angels showing themselves before the Lord, and Satan is with them.

He has been reduced to wreaking havoc on the earth for the past 6,000 years or so, and will continue to do this until God locks him up for good. Part of this havoc-wreaking response is loading up the world with false gods. Because we are born with the transmitted sin nature imbedded in us, we are born therefore natural enemies of God. That makes it very difficult to sift through all of the fallacious gods and goddesses that we have been hearing and learning about since nursery school, and cut to the truth.

Years ago I was told by someone involved about one of the challenges he and other scientists and engineers faced who were innovators in the Strategic Defense Initiative (SDI), dubbed "Star Wars."

The intent of SDI was to develop an anti-ballistic missile system that could take out nuclear warheads that were launched against our country. It got the nickname "Star Wars" because of the planned space-based and ground-based nuclear X-ray lasers, subatomic particle beams, and computer-guided projectiles fired by electromagnetic rail guns that were proposed.

They determined that once a nuclear attack was initiated against us, they had less than twenty-five minutes from the time the missiles left earth's atmosphere until they reentered the atmosphere over the USA. During that twenty-five minute window, they had to identify and destroy each nuclear warhead.

They had already developed defense weapons that were capable of destroying nuclear warheads while they were still in space, which would minimize damage on earth. The problem was that, during an attack, the enemy was prepared to deploy numerous decoys and our computers had to somehow be able to distinguish between what was a real warhead and what was a dummy. Their concern was that there would not be enough time (twenty-five minutes) to identify and destroy them all. The realization was that many nuclear warheads would get through.

Which God Should I Choose?

Satan has deployed numerous decoys at our world with the intention of minimizing our ability to identify the one true God. Some of them are very convincing imitations.

When I was a teenager, quite a large group of friends and I made plans to go duck hunting. Somebody's friend's uncle owned a hunting camp somewhere on Lake Champlain, so, after work that Friday, we headed north.

After a few hours' drive, we had to park the car and take a boat the rest of the way to the secluded camp. It was quite adventurous and very exciting. We arrived at the cabin a while before dark, so my two closest hunting buddies and I decided to check out a bay we were told about that was about a half hours' hike away.

When we got there, it looked like a really good spot for ducks to fly in. There was nothing going on then, but we made plans to head back there early the next morning. When we got back to the cabin, a few other guys had showed up and the party had begun.

As it got later, I tried to talk my two friends into turning in, but they wanted no part of it. Around midnight I took my sleeping bag, went out to a front room and tried to sleep amidst a very great noise.

Almost like part of a cruel nightmare, my alarm woke me up at 5:00 AM. I got up very grudgingly and, as I staggered through the camp, there were bodies strewn everywhere. I shook my friends as I found them and tried to wake them up to go, but they were more like unconscious than asleep.

Dejected, I decided I would have to go alone. I walked over to a window and peered out, trying to plan my next move. It was a very beautiful morning. There was no sun yet, but it was getting lighter. There was a mist rising off from the lake. The water was very still

The God Of This World

and placid, as smooth as glass. It was a very moving sight.

I looked down the hill that led from the front porch to a little cove about fifty feet away. Startled, I sucked in a quick gulp of air and my heart stopped. My eyes opened wide and my mouth dropped as my head leaned forward a little. My heart began beating again, now pounding. There in the water, right below me, were a half a dozen ducks that apparently had flown in during the night!

My heart was beating hard and I began to tremble a little. As quietly and slowly as I could, I backed away from the window, kind of like tiptoeing backwards.

I crept to my friend Hance and shook him rather violently. "Hance, Hance," I whispered loudly. He peered up at me as I exclaimed, "There's ducks down in the cove!"

He mumbled something and closed his eyes.

Somewhere in the camp though, somebody yelled, "Shut up, will ya?"

I froze. The ducks would hear us. I couldn't risk trying to wake up Hance or Mur (my other friend) anymore. I slowly moved to where my stuff was. Gently, I unzipped my gun case and slid out my shotgun. I was shaking pretty good as I loaded three shells. A pump shotgun makes all kinds of noise when you pump a shell into the chamber, so I moved the action very slowly, not breathing as I pulled the pump handle down and then pushed it back up again. Even going slowly, it made what seemed to me like deafening clicking sounds.

Done loading, I blew out a nervous breath and inched my way to the door that opened onto the front porch. I crouched down by door and turned the handle. I started to pull the door open and immediately froze. It squeaked! I couldn't believe it. I had to move the door a tiny bit at a time until it was open enough for me to crawl through.

I crawled on my stomach across the length of the porch to the door that opened towards the cove. As I got to the door, holding my breath, I slowly rose up, moved the curtain and peered out the glass. The ducks were still there!

I lowered back down and, with my stomach on the floor, turned the doorknob and started very carefully opening the door, still not breathing. I pushed the door out inch by inch until I could see the cove, and then snuck my gun barrel through the opening.

BANG! BANG! ... BANG!

My ears were ringing now along with my pounding heart as I stood to my feet and pushed the door fully open. As I peered out through the smoke filled air at the cove below, very surprisingly, at least some of the ducks were still there. I was in a mild state of confusion at that point and started to panic a little because I hadn't brought anymore shotgun shells out to the porch with me.

What happened next is hard to imagine unless you have stayed up most of the night, fallen asleep in a small cabin with no electricity, bathroom, or insulation, in the middle of nowhere, and then been abruptly awakened at 5:30 AM by three blasts from a 12 gauge magnum shotgun no more than twenty-five feet away from where you were sleeping.

I was thinking about running back to my knapsack and reloading, but at that same moment the small cabin had erupted into a bit of pandemonium. Several guys were running around inside the camp trying to figure out what had happened, and a few came hurrying out onto the porch. I was kind of glad to see that everyone was finally awake. They were yelling something about

The God Of This World

what was going on, but I was more concerned about the fact that there were still ducks down there and my need for more ammo.

One of the guys marched past me and looked out the door, down toward the cove below. "Those are decoys, you idiot!" he said very harshly.

Puzzled, I thought hard for a second, then looked past him down at the water and said, "What?" in kind of a slow, stumped voice.

One by one, everyone started walking away, shaking their heads, and mumbling. I stood there by myself, looking down at the decoys and thinking, *Decoys... really?*

I was demoralized. How could I have been that positive of something and still be wrong?

As I reflect back, I was totally convinced that those decoys were real ducks. And since I had no useful prior information, what other conclusion could I have drawn? It was early morning at a duck hunting camp, it was duck season, and they were acting like what I thought ducks should act like. If I was a little more experienced, I may have known that ducks don't just sit in a group with one another and not move, and would have been a little more suspicious of these. Also, if someone had told me that I should expect to see decoys out in front of the cabin that morning, I would have been aware of the possibility.

Without warnings and prior knowledge, falling for a false god can happen in a very similar way. Many times false gods disguise themselves to look like what people think God should really look like. Their leaders resemble genuinely godly people and their followers are very persuasive. Unknowingly, people can become convinced in their own minds quite easily that the god they are following is the right one without any proof whatsoever. Then, without being aware of their mistake, they in turn try to pass their beliefs on to others.

For many of us, it's a lot like this when we're trying to choose the right God. The enemy has launched several false gods at us, and it can be very difficult to figure out which one is real. As a result, we may choose one just because it's the one that's on our path in life. If you're born into a Mormon household, chances are you may follow the Mormon god because that's the way you were brought up. If you're Japanese, you may feel Buddhism or Shintoism is the direction you should lean. Years ago, I was talking to one of the guys at work about God. He clearly didn't want anything to do with God, but did share with me that he was an Episcopalian. He said he really didn't know what that meant, but his father was one, so he figured he must be one too.

How and where we're brought up can certainly lead us in a particular direction concerning which god we worship or believe in. This can also be extremely unfortunate if our family, friends, or culture are following the wrong god.

You may be reading this book because you have concerns about the god your family or friends are following. Up until now, you've been playing along, but it has become apparent that something is either wrong or missing. That often happens. Children usually grow up following their parents' faith and rarely develop a faith of their own. This can be true of both families who are following the *wrong* god as well as families who are following the *right* God. In the case of a family member whose parents are following the wrong god, this can be a good thing. At least you are open to checking it out and seeing if somebody you know might be making a mistake.

Another tragic scenario is when children are brought up in homes where there is abuse, neglect, alcoholism, hypocrisy, divorce, and so on. They don't like what they see in their parents and want nothing to do with their religion or god. Since most religions seem similar on the surface, children associate the real God with their parents' religion and end up not wanting anything to do with God. They have no idea that the god their parents have been displaying to them is not the real God at all.

It is possible though, with prior warning through good advice, that they may be able to know what to look for in order to avoid such a trap. That's why it's so important to get whatever information is available and examine all the facts surrounding the many choices. Being sure, which is built on emotions, is not the same as knowing for sure, which is built on facts.

It is true that duck decoys are not supposed to attract unsuspecting hunters, but they are supposed to fool ducks. Unsuspecting ducks see friendly, happy-looking ducks seemingly enjoying a safe and peaceful haven, when all the time they are being lured into a trap.

My intention is to share truths and verifiable facts that I have gathered through careful research concerning the different choices that are out there so that you can make an educated decision.

Being aware of the characteristics of the decoys will help, but it would be far better to study the real God and find out everything you can about Him. Knowing what something real looks like always makes it easier to spot a phony. Studying the Bible is, without question, the most certain method you can use to help you get to know the real God.

Listen carefully to wisdom; set your mind on understanding. Cry out for wisdom, and beg for understanding. Search for it like silver, and hunt for it like hidden treasure. Then you will understand respect for the Lord, and you will find that you know God.

~Proverbs 2:2-5

Chapter Eleven

ANOTHER GOD WORTH MENTIONING

> God's work of refining and purifying the soul must go on until his servants are so humbled, so dead to self, that when called into active service, they may have an eye single to the glory of God.
> ~Ellen G. White (1827-1915)[47]

Although this may sound boring or unlikely at first, one of the biggest "gods" that people around the world follow after doesn't really have a name. It is more like a category. In this category of things that people worship (or live for—what we live for is what we worship) are money, pleasure, and pride (power and fame).

Doing evil and wanting evil things, thinking evil thoughts, sexual sins, and greed are all a part of the worship services for this false god (Colossians 3:5-6). It's a "god of self" kind of religion. These devoted followers of themselves put themselves first in everything, and everything or everyone else takes a back seat. Obviously, this god of self has to worship these other things (money, pleasure, and pride) as well, in order for it to survive.

Since there is only one true God, if we — as part of the creation of that one real God — put anything else ahead of Him, then that thing, in effect, becomes our god. We may not see it that way, but God does.

If our child starts spending all their time with the neighbor's parent, seeking and following their advice, wanting to always be with them, wanting to be like them, even loving them, how would that make us feel? If you're not a parent yet, then you may not be able to fully relate to this favoritism, so what if you were still a child and your parents poured all their interest into the child of someone else, investing all of their time, money, love and devotion into this other child, and wanting nothing to do with you? Either way, hopefully you can see that the one who is supposed to be the object of our devotion is being ignored.

And that's the way it is with God when His creation follows after other gods, whether it's self (the worship of what we see, what we feel, and our own pride), or a full-blown false entity such as any of the numerous false gods in our world today.

THE LUST OF THE EYES

> Too many people spend money they earned ... to buy things they don't want ... to impress people that they don't like.
> ~Will Rogers (1879-1935)

Perhaps you've heard the saying that the love of money is the root of all evil. If money is your god, then this is definitely the case. Wherever there is evil afoot, money will not be far away. Those who love money will do just about anything to get it. There is a verse in the Bible that asks what profit is it if you gain the whole world and lose your own soul? That's a good question—with a bad answer.

It should be noted that there are positives and negatives with money. On the negative side, money's promises are empty. If you think more money will end your problems, be wary. More money ends many problems— it's true—but it can create many more than it ends if money is your god.

I have worked for some very rich people. Many millionaires, and even a billionaire. I can tell you with certainty that having a billion dollars does not end financial worries. The billionaire that I worked for had a different set of financial problems than I have. Different, and much bigger. Although most of these rich employers were nice enough people, I would categorize them as pretty much miserable.

The trouble with having so much money is that you realize money isn't the answer at all. It doesn't give you peace, happiness, or contentment, the three things that people are wanting the most. Many people have climbed the ladder to success only to find that when they got to the top, there was nothing completely satisfying there. One billionaire was asked, "How much more do you need?" His answer: "Just a little more." Another, who owned a professional baseball team and a television super station, stated that he was the most miserable man who ever lived.

The problem is this. You may spend a major portion of your life giving all your time and effort, sacrificing your family, your friends, and maybe even your own good name—maybe even your own soul—striving to acquire great wealth for yourself, because that has always been the goal. Then, when you finally get there, it's only to find that it's not worth what you thought it was worth. It's not worth what you had to give up in order to get it.

If this was the lifelong goal, and if this was all that was or all that had ever been important, and it turns out to be a disappointment, what do you do next? Getting a lot of money and enjoying life was the dream. Unfortunately, it just doesn't happen that way. It's more like a nightmare. People who reach that goal find that they used to be dissatisfied with little money, and now are dissatisfied with a lot of money. So, money, in and of itself, is not the answer. Money is not the real God.

> Don't wear yourself out trying to get rich; be wise enough to control yourself. Wealth can vanish in the wink of an eye. It can seem to grow wings and fly away like an eagle.
> ~Proverbs 23:3-4

Another negative with money is that it can disappear as quickly as it came, or in most cases, quicker. If you put your hope and trust in uncertain riches, you will ultimately be very disappointed. The book of Proverbs in the Bible cautions not to wear yourself out trying to get rich, because money can seem to grow wings and fly away like an eagle.

I mentioned above that oftentimes, most people who gain wealth are dissatisfied and miserable. On the other side of that coin, however, there are those who bury themselves in luxury and enjoy it to the max. There are, of course, problems even then. For one, they will have to fight hard, seemingly nonstop, in order to remain flush, and, even though some are fortunate enough to hold on to their fortunes until the end, when money is all there is, the end is not all that savory.

On his deathbed, while being interviewed by a reporter and asked to sum up his life, Clarence Darrow, one of the most famous American lawyers of all time, said, "My colleagues say that I am a success. Many honors have come my way, but in the Bible is a sentence that expresses the way I feel about life: 'We have toiled all night and taken nothing.'" Even though he took this Bible verse out of context, it demonstrates that Clarence Darrow at least realized at the end of his life that the success, fame, power, and money he had amassed had been all for nothing.

> Wealth inherited quickly in the beginning will do you no good in the end.
> ~Proverbs 20:21

Studies show that instant wealth, in most cases, is worse that no wealth at all. The other day I heard about a lottery winner who was in trouble with the law, so I Googled "lottery winners in prison." Surprisingly enough (to me), I got 92,800,000 results. Of note, one woman kept collecting food stamps after winning millions. Several were jailed for welfare fraud, others were convicted of drug trafficking, prostitution, possession of illegal firearms, tax fraud and tax evasion, and many, almost unbelievably, have been convicted of murder. And that was just the first page. One guy tried to strangle his girlfriend to death because she was spending too much money. Another man plotted to have his brother killed (who had actually won the millions) in hopes of inheriting his fortune.

And lottery winners don't just end up in prison. Most who don't go to jail either end up broke, bankrupt, losing their friends and family, developing huge gambling and/or drug addictions, going into hiding, committing suicide, or experiencing other equally tragic outcomes. Nearly all, at one point or another, end up regretting that they ever won the money in the first place.

It isn't just lottery winners who experience tragedy when they get rich quick. Professional sports stars, in many instances, become millionaires almost overnight. In most cases, they have little education and no idea whatsoever how to handle money, even though it has been the dream to acquire it all along. In fact, 60 percent of all National Basketball Association players are broke or in financial trouble within five years of retiring from the sport. Even more concerning is that 78 percent of all National Football League players suffer the same ill fate within *two* years of their retirement. Broke. Nearly as fast as it came, it's gone. In fact, many go bust while they are still playing.[48] No wonder they hold out for more money. It seems it really doesn't matter how much money they hold out for, or how long they hold out for it—it's all going to be gone in a few years anyway.

Although there are many other categories of people groups enduring bad fortune, we will finish this section with celebrities. When you hear names like Burt Reynolds, Nicholas Cage, Kevin Bacon, M. C. Hammer, Jerry Lee Lewis, Wayne Newton, David Crosby, Marvin Gaye, Willie Nelson, or Michael Jackson mentioned as people who are broke or in financial crisis, you have to wonder. Of course, Michael Jackson died, but not before losing his famous multimillion-dollar Neverland ranch to foreclosure and the prized money rights to the entire Beatles music collection in settlement.

It's depressing to think about, so imagine how it feels. Putting your hope and trust in something that is bound to disappear is not wise, but for a majority of people, money is their god.

> Riches gotten by doing wrong have no value, but right living will save you from death.
>
> ~Proverbs 10:2

So far, we've looked at many different kinds of rich people who have shown a total disregard for the real God and worshiped their money instead. Does this mean you have to be rich in order to have money as your god? Absolutely not. Many people who are not considered financially well-off still worship money, and this in turn leads to all kinds of evildoing. This is not surprising if you consider that, in the Bible (which many consider to be God's Word), it states that "the love of money causes all kinds of evil."

There are 6 million people in American prisons today. That's staggering when you think about it. Statistically, that means that there are roughly 760 prisoners per every 100,000 US citizens, or seven out of every 1,000 people in America are in jail.[49] It is not a long shot to say that most of them were not rich just prior to committing their crimes. If the love of money is at the heart of most evil, then you would have to believe that money — and, in fact, the love of money — was involved in the events that led to the incarceration of the majority of these 6 million people in one way or another.

Whether rich or poor, people will do just about anything to get or keep money. Anything that is, except put their trust in God. Putting our trust in God to help us out financially can't sound like that crazy of a notion, in light of the fact that every single dollar I have ever owned has "In God We Trust" printed on it. Money itself tries to teach us that it is not what we are supposed to put our trust in.

So, with a little money or a bunch of money, there are still problems, worries, and frustrations. Either way, there is an emptiness that cannot be filled, and whether one is a billionaire or a low-income laborer, they can be happy one minute and sad the next.

Therefore, if there's relatively the same degree of happiness with money or without money, then it's obviously not the real God and not worth devoting our existence to. The real God will allow you to devote your existence to whatever you choose, but He will only be pleased if you choose to devote it to Him. The real God will teach you to be content with whatever you have, whether a little or a lot. At that point you will notice that you have a peace in your heart that others cannot understand and find that you are beginning to live life more abundantly.

Until we learn that, the quest for more money will consume us, and no matter how much we have, it will never be enough.

> Don't envy sinners but always respect the Lord, then you will have hope for the future, and your wishes will come true.
> ~Proverbs 23:17-18

On the other hand, I have also met many millionaires whose God is the real God and whose money is a useful tool for them. When this priority is straight, that's when the peace, contentment, and joy that this world can afford comes in.

You must realize that God is in control of everything. He decides how much money you will have and how long you will have it. If you worship it, it will be gone. If you worship Him, He will provide for all your needs. If you trust in Him, He will give you lasting success and will make your wishes come true.

Money can be a useful tool for all who trust in God,

when dealt with properly. Whether rich or poor, the one who believes and trusts in the real God will have all the money they need for whatever situation God has planned for them to need it for. There are a lot of positive things that can be done with money. You can either do a lot to build up things for yourself with money, or you can do a lot to build up things for God. It comes down to each individual's choice.

Don't get me wrong. God does not need your money. God owns everything there is, whether seen or unseen. What God wants is your heart (the inner part of you that is who you really are), and where your heart is, your money will not be far behind.

> Ignorance breeds monsters to fill up the vacancies of the soul that are occupied by the verities of knowledge.
> ~Horace Mann, "The Father of American Education" (1796-1859)

I'm not completely sure what is at the heart of bringing immorality to the surface in a person's life. I am taught that it is imbedded in each one of us at birth, but it is noticeably suppressed, at least opportunely, by some more than others.

What starts it? What drives it? I've heard over the years that viewing pornography at a young age sets the stage for an immoral life. That can be concerning.

When I was growing up in the 1960s, pornography, at least for a young teen, was not all that easy to come by. I was probably twelve or thirteen at the time of my first experience with it, and truthfully, it was quite by accident.

There were some overgrown dirt path-type roads just a few hundred yards out behind my house that

Which God Should I Choose?

wound down through the woods to a stream. (Reflecting back, I guess they were probably old, abandoned logging roads.) The older kids in my neighborhood always had a field car back there that they would bomb around in, running up and down the trails until the car died, crashed, or rolled over, at which point they would abandon it and find another.

They had a primitive plywood shack that was their clubhouse/hangout. It was somewhat hidden off one of the trails. It was called, at least by my friends, "the car lot." As I was growing up, it was more like a legend. I had heard about it, but had never seen it.

Never, that is, until one fateful fall day, some friends and I were down exploring in the woods when we chanced upon it. Someone had broken the lock and left the door open. So, we went in. As we rummaged around (and it was nasty in there), under an old, rotten mattress, we found a pile of damp, moldy, black and white porn magazines. The pages were pretty much stuck together and deteriorated, but we could see enough.

It was a life-changing experience for sure, but that was pretty much the end of it. We went back again to the shack one more time, but the magazines were gone. I didn't have any older brothers or older friends. I only had three black and white network television channels and as far as I know, my father did not have such things, so access to pornography was extremely limited.

> God's plan made a hopeful beginning. But man spoiled his chances by sinning. We trust that the story will end in God's glory. But, at present, the other side's winning.
> ~Oliver Wendell Holmes,
> American author and poet (1809-1894)

Another God Worth Mentioning

Fast forward to today, and the tides have turned. Access to pornography on the Internet is truly unbelievable. Unless you understand what terabytes and petrabytes are, you probably will not be able to grasp in computer language the amount of pornographic material that is viewed on the Internet every day.

According to Extremetech.com, there are dozens of porn sites that are up to three times larger than CNN or ESPN, and hundreds more that are as large as your favorite news site. Each site has up to 100 million page visits per day, which adds up to billions and billions of views per month that last on average around fifteen to twenty minutes each. Thirty percent of all web traffic goes to pornography websites, 372 people per second search Google for porn sites, and 400 new porn sites are added to the Internet on average per day.

According to a recent survey commissioned by HP and conducted by Wakefield Research, children ages six to seventeen spend at least three hours per day on devices with Internet access, in part because computers have taken on a significant role in homework assignments for students as young as ten years old. Of these, 66 percent *do not* use parental controls or block websites deemed inappropriate.[50]

That's why I mentioned earlier that it's concerning if viewing pornography at a young age may be what sets the stage for living an immoral life.

I was talking to a friend of mine awhile back, and he shared with me in tears that while his four young children were home after school, one was researching something on the Internet as part of their homework. The child accidentally typed in the wrong website address and was directed to an illicit pornographic website. There, in his own living room, his children observed things that he had hoped they would never see, even as adults. I have to imagine, as children, once you see these things, you are never really the same again.

How do you get those images out of your mind? I would guess — and it can't sound all that far-fetched, looking at the statistics — that without some kind of therapy or counseling, coupled with an accountability relationship with someone not involved in immorality, you can't. And in most cases, without help, once you have you have trodden down this path, whether accidentally or on purpose, you will eventually, and not accidentally, find your way back.

I know you can't hit a rewind, backspace, or erase button and start over, so the experience, with all its filthy, vivid images, will be lodged somewhere in your memory for a very long time — probably the rest of your life.

All is not lost though. There is hope. Chances are, many of you who are reading this book will have to sadly admit that you have been and are now involved with pornography of one form or another. I don't want you to feel like you've been condemned already and there's no way out. Or that there's no chance for recovery, forgiveness, and a fresh start. That's another merciful characteristic of the real God. He is willing to forgive and forget things such as this if we are willing to forsake them altogether.

And, like any addiction, it is possible to conquer this one. Plus, once conquered, it is possible to suppress those memories and keep them so far down in the back of your mind that they will rarely, if ever, surface again. That is yet another benefit of choosing the right God; He will help you battle the addiction and suppress the memories once you turn to Him. The real God is a God who wants to help you fix the things in your life that are wrong.

But, without a doubt, the very best bet is to never get those images in your mind in the first place and not allow yourself to become addicted to them. And they are positively as addicting as any addiction that a person can succumb to. (I refer you back to the staggering statistics.) As much as it is possible, you should do whatever it takes to protect yourself, your spouse, and your children from this invasion of their morality. Like a guard dog, watch over your family's Internet activity. Talk it over with them. Tell them how concerned you are for their moral well-being. Explain to them the dangers and enlist their help in blocking this foe from your home.

Of course, the Internet is not the only danger we face. Immorality is a minefield in life that we must traipse through. There should be major concerns about movies, television, books, magazines, and music videos that can all be invasive to our search for the right God and our walk with Him, once we find Him.

There are approximately 11,000 pornographic movies released each year on DVD. That, of course, doesn't count movies that contain immoral content, which may be too numerous to count. On top of that, there are many television programs and many music videos that should be avoided at all costs. If you watch them, they will stain you.

I know of several families who have done away with television in their homes. For some, that's just not an option. I salute the ones who have, because that is probably the best way to eliminate one more source of temptation from your family's presence. If you're like me though, and can't imagine not having a television, there are safeguards you can employ that will block or filter much of the immoral content according to what you decide is suitable. We use TVGuardian® for filtering swearing out of TV shows, and ClearPlay™ for filtering swearing and immorality out of movies. They're not free, but they are an investment into the morality of your family.

TVGuardian® is a one-time purchase. It is a small box that you run your HD satellite or cable feeds through on the way to your television. It basically mutes profanity while you're watching TV and movies according to your preferred filter level.

ClearPlay™ is a little more involved. You have to purchase the ClearPlay™ DVD player, and then download filters onto a USB flash drive. The filters load for each movie before you start watching them. You have to load new filters from the ClearPlay™ website as new movies are released, and you have to pay a monthly payment for the service. In my estimation, if you like to watch movies, it is well worth the price. In fact, what price can you put on something that takes the immorality out of the eyes and ears of your children and teaches them at the same time that those things are wrong and should be removed?

> Imagination is a God-given gift; but if it is fed dirt by the eye, it will be dirty. All sin, not least sexual sin, begins with the imagination. Therefore what feeds the imagination is of maximum importance in the pursuit of kingdom righteousness.
> ~D.A. Carson, Author

THE LUST OF THE FLESH

I ask different ones their opinions on whether they think alcohol or drugs may play into the dramatic rise of immorality in the world today and people's seemingly insatiable desire for pornography. For the most part, the answer is the same: "Probably, yes." I doubt that everyone who is involved with pornography uses alcohol and drugs, *but* I do think it's possible that the majority of people who do use alcohol and drugs may not mind viewing pornography.

It's hard to say which is increasing more rapidly—alcohol and drug abuse, or indulgence in pornography. The beer manufacturing industry reports selling 211,489,982 barrels of beer a year. That boils down to 71,060,633,952 twelve-ounce bottles of beer a year. For those of you that are not all that good with long numbers, that's well over 71 billion bottles of beer sold each year. According to the Census Bureau, that's twenty-two gallons worth of beer per person in America. Now, because many of us, including young children, don't drink, that means somebody else is drinking my twenty-two gallons on top of their own, and probably a lot of somebodies. Americans also drink on average two and a half gallons of wine and a proportionate amount of liquor each year as well. And again, somebody somewhere is drinking my share, as well as their own.[51]

In fact, according to an annual Gallup survey, 66 percent of Americans reported that they consume alcohol occasionally. Of these, about half said they drank one to seven drinks the week prior to the survey, while 12 percent said they drink eight or more. Furthermore, 22 percent of those who drink alcoholic beverages admitted that they sometimes drink too much. Beyond that, it is estimated that 13.8 million Americans develop problems associated with alcohol consumption.

These figures may be low, as Learn-About-Alcoholism.com reports that three-fourths of all American adults drink alcohol.[52] Since there are roughly

315 million people living in America right now, that's about 237 million people. Of these, over 12 million are estimated to be alcoholics.

> Public schools are the nurseries of all vice and immorality.
> ~Henry Fielding,
> British Playwright and Novelist (1707-1754)

In today's teenage population, over 90 percent have used alcohol. In fact, according to the Center For Disease Control, 11 percent of all people who drink are between the ages of twelve and twenty. That can mean more than 8 billion bottles of beer earmarked annually just for kids twelve to twenty years old, plus a proportionate amount of wine and liquor.

And also, according to the CDC, 90 percent of all teenage alcohol consumption is in the form of binge drinking. That means, according to statistical information, approximately 81 percent of all teenagers in America have indulged in binge drinking.

Binge drinking basically means you drink so much that when (and if, because some kids die from it) you wake up the next morning, you don't know who you ended up with, where you were, or what you did. According to the CDC, binge drinking is associated with unintentional injuries such as car crashes, falls, burns, and drowning. Intentional injuries include firearm injuries, sexual assault, and domestic violence.

Other issues associated with binge drinking include alcohol poisoning, sexually transmitted diseases, unintended pregnancy, high blood pressure, strokes, liver disease, neurological damage, sexual dysfunction, and poor control of diabetes.

While teens drinking alcohol present all kinds of

Another God Worth Mentioning

horrors on its own, over 50 percent have used marijuana, 17 percent admit to trying cocaine and 12.5 percent have used some form of hallucinogen.[53] Sadly, on average, 11,318 teens try alcohol for the first time each day. These teens are four times more likely to become alcoholics than those who wait until they are twenty-one to start drinking. Three-fourths of all high school students report being drunk at least once. That's upwards of 13,500,000 students every year. (Thirteen and a half a million!)

In the year 2000, seven million kids between the ages of twelve and twenty were binge drinkers. By 2007, that figure had grown to 7.2 million. I would guess that number may have risen higher by today, as now, teens are mixing alcohol with energy drinks, which according to experts, makes them three times more likely to binge drink.[54]

> God made husbands and wives to become one body and one spirit for his purpose—so they would have children who are true to God.
> ~Malachi 2:15

One thing is clear. As we are deciding which god we should choose, we need to also take into consideration the future of our children. Whichever god we choose, our children may choose to follow as well. So, we need to also ask ourselves, which god will also be right for them?

I don't know for sure if Henry Fielding was right, and if he was, what anyone could do about it. There are a couple things I do know that directly correlate with this depressing information. As bad as public schools may have been in the 1700s all the way through the 1950s, by the early 1960s things became dramatically worse in

American schools. In 1962, the US Supreme Court began the removal from public schools of the very God, of all the gods, that we should choose. It established what is now the current prohibition on state-sponsored prayer within the public school system.[55] In 1963 it was decided by the court that Bible readings and other school-sponsored religious activities should be prohibited. The effects these decisions have had on young people's pursuit of the god of immorality are paramount.

Numerous studies have shown that up until 1962 most immoral activity in America remained, on average, at about the same rate year after year. After 1962, all categories of immoral and unlawful activity imaginable began increasing at alarming rates. You really don't have to investigate too deeply to see that there is a serious moral problem that is not going away.

If nothing else, the statistics prove that the God who was removed from the presence of the children of America is a God who is able to battle the god of immorality and keep him in check. Once this moral God was removed, the god of immorality has been able to run rampant in our nation's schools.

It seems obvious that immorality is a depraved, sinful condition that leads only to pain and eventual heartache. The immoral person defines morality by his or her own set of standards that are based solely on what they feel, think, or believe to be true. Their truth is not based on facts, but on personal, selfish desires.

Any god that is involved in any form of immoral activity, therefore, cannot be the true God, because God is morally pure. Remember Webster's definition of God, "perfect in goodness." Perfect is defined as absolutely flawless or pure. I'm hoping that with all of this information you will be able to see clearly that any god involved in immoral activities cannot be the right

God to choose, and of all the gods, the field can now be narrowed down to only those gods that are moral and just. As we sift a little further through what's left once we've removed the immoral gods from the equation, it should become apparent that only one God out of any remaining gods truly possesses all of the characteristics and virtues of a real God.

> My experience through life has convinced me that, while moderation and temperance in all things are commendable and beneficial, abstinence from spirituous liquors is the best safeguard of morals and health.
> ~Robert E. Lee (1807-1870)

Going back to the original question of the possibility that alcohol or drug consumption may be linked with immorality, statistics show that alcohol is a factor in 41 percent of all rape cases alone. In addition, more than 60 percent of college girls who have contracted sexually transmitted diseases, herpes, or AIDS were intoxicated at the time of infection.[53]

According to ezinearticles.com, alcohol and adultery go together like bread and butter. They believe that most cases of adulterous activity would not happen if alcohol were not involved. Ehow.com agrees by saying that people under the influence of drugs or alcohol are much more like to commit adultery than those who are not. It's hard to argue with that, especially when examiner.com states that up to 50 percent of all affairs involve alcohol during their indiscretions.[56]

Alcohol, of course, is a legal drug. Being legal, however, does not make it either smart nor safe. On top of being the most widely used drug in America, it is also the most widely abused.

As far as illegal drugs go, it is estimated that 22.5 million Americans ages twelve or older are illicit drug users. This figure represents 8.7 percent of the American population ages twelve or older. These illicit drugs include, but are surely not limited to (as new drugs are invented every day), marijuana, hash, cocaine (including crack), heroin, hallucinogens, inhalants, or prescription psychotherapeutics (pain relievers, tranquilizers, stimulants, and sedatives) used nonmedically.[57] Drug use in any form, legal or illegal, is bound to impair our moral judgment and loosen whatever self-control we may maintain. If you have never tried any of these drugs (alcohol included), then I encourage you to: one, believe that what I am saying is factual, and two, never do. If you have partaken in any of the drugs mentioned above (including alcohol), then deep down inside you know that what I am saying is true, and once you come to the realization that there is a God, He cannot possibly be found associated with those things or involved with them.

> Do not be lazy but work hard, serving the Lord with all your heart.
> ~Romans 12:11

I am not a psychologist so am not sure why so many people bury themselves in their work. Maybe it is greed for more money that drives a person, or maybe it's just simply an insatiable desire to work. It could be a result of boredom, loneliness, fear, or even the need of a refuge. People work for a variety of reasons and—in fact—God wants us to work and earn what we need.

Working, therefore, is good. The problem begins when we become obsessed with our work. You've probably heard of the term *workaholic*. Rodney Dangerfield said, "My old man was a workaholic: every time he thought about work, he got drunk." That's funny and tragic at the same time, but not entirely accurate. The true definition of a workaholic is quite a bit more serious and has no humor involved in it at all. Merely tragedy.

A workaholic is defined as one who is obsessively addicted to work—and probably sometimes, but not necessarily always, alcohol, too (my observation).

In order to find the satisfaction we all desire and seek, there has to be a proper balance between God, your family, and your work. Each one deserves your time, but it is not healthy or wise to devote unbalanced time to any one of these priorities (especially work). Many people do make work their god, but in the end, it never pays off.

It is most important to put God first in your life, have God as the center of your family, and do your work diligently, as if you are working directly for the Lord. When we devote too much time to any one of the three, however, it will be at the expense of another.

Normally (not always), once work becomes your god, the next thing to go is the family. No matter what occupation you are in, neglected family members are not going to do well on their own. Spouses will become resentful and distant, while children become rebellious and wayward. Families are hard to hold together and fall apart quite easily. They require an equal portion of our time, but, in almost all circumstances of an unbalanced life, families are what take the big hit, while work is the ultimate winner.

THE RESULT

My wife Mary and I have been married for forty-seven years and not once have we had an

argument serious enough to consider divorce; ...
murder, yes, but divorce, never.
~Jack Benny (1894-1974)

According to numerous reports and statistics, the divorce rate is much higher in marriages with at least one spouse being over-absorbed in work. One study by UK management consultant Grant Thorton concluded that, among the main causes for divorce in 2004, 6 percent was attributed to excessive work habits by one of the partners. In 70 percent of those divorces, it was the man who was at fault.[58] A more recent study shows that work-related divorces have now tripled. In fact, according to an article by Roger Dobson and Ed Habershon, among couples who have divorced recently, 28 percent of the women polled mentioned excessive working hours in their motives.[59]

Obviously, there are many causes for divorce besides excessively working, including the love of money which we have previously examined. And, in fact, there can be multiple irreconcilable differences in the same divorce battle. As bad as divorce is on the surface—both in the eyes of God and for the man and woman involved—the problems run much deeper. Divorce can very easily disrupt many more than just two lives at a time.

> Others are like the seed planted among the thorny weeds. They hear the teaching, but the worries of this life, the temptation of wealth, and many other evil desires keep the teaching from growing and producing fruit in their lives.
> ~Mark 4:18

The statistics concerning children in families of divorced parents are shocking. Since the real God is the One who originally designed and instituted marriage and the family, I can't imagine He is thrilled by the impact divorce has on the kids. Although what happens to children in a broken family is not a crime as far as the laws of man are concerned, it probably should be.

Believe it or not, it is estimated that half of all American children alive today will witness the breakup up of their parents' marriage. Also, at this moment, 40 percent of all American children are being raised without their father living at home. Sixty-three percent (63%) of youth suicides, 90 percent of all homeless and runaway children, 85 percent of all children exhibiting behavioral disorders, 80 percent of rapists motivated by displaced anger, 71 percent of all high school dropouts, 75 percent of all adolescent patients in chemical abuse centers, 70 percent of juveniles in state-operated institutions, and 85 percent of all youths in prisons grew up in father-deprived homes.[60]

Statistics also show that children in a female-headed home are ten times more likely to be beaten or murdered. Children living in a single parent home have about the same likelihood of being the victim of child molestation as do children of drug ring leaders. Teenagers from single parent families or blended families are three times more likely to need psychological help than those living with their two real parents at home.

Children of divorced parents are more likely to experience injury, asthma, headaches, and speech defects, and are 50 percent more likely to develop some kind of health problem than children living at home with their two parents. These children living with their two parents are twenty to thirty-five percent more healthy than children with divorced parents.

Furthermore, of all the children born to married parents this year, 50 percent will witness the divorce of their parents before their eighteenth birthday. Multiply that by the following eighteen years, and by that time, the number of children under the age of eighteen being the product of a broken home will be unimaginable. The long-term effects on children of divorced parents are equally disturbing. Studies show that even after six years, children from divorced parents tend to be lonely, unhappy, anxious, and insecure. Sadly, they are two times more likely to drop out of school, two times more likely to attempt suicide, and teenage girls are two times more likely to become pregnant.

The problems do not end when these children reach adulthood either, for 70 percent of long-term prison inmates grew up in broken homes.[61]

According to the FBI, the crime rate has increased 158 percent since 1960. This is almost precisely the result to be expected from correlating the divorce rate with broken home/delinquency rates, proving that the roots develop in childhood. Dr. Shervert H. Frazier, in a study of convicted murderers in Texas prisons and mental institutions, has this to say: "They are males with an absence of a father symbol."[62]

According to numerous studies, adults who were children of broken homes are more likely to have children out of wedlock, end up in jail, live in poverty, and develop sociopathic behavior. Also, they are less likely to marry, more likely to divorce, and more likely to become angry and violent.

The workaholic lifestyle is becoming a bigger problem each year in the United States. According to the Bureau of Labor Statistics, there are an estimated 10 million workers who average more than sixty hours per week.[63] 10 million! That's a huge number of people who have no room in their lives for anything more than work.

Besides abandoning their families and increasing the risk of divorce, workaholics live a very unhealthy way of life. Research shows that they have a significantly higher than average incidence of stress-related illnesses and alcohol abuse.[64]

As further proof of the workaholic lifestyle problem, more Americans are canceling their vacations each year. According to a *USA Today* survey, 64 percent of Americans canceled their vacations in 2010. One-third cancel their vacations due to work-related reasons, 25 percent check into work regularly while on vacation, and 58 percent feel they are more in need of a vacation than last year.[65]

> Let parents bequeath to their children not riches, but the spirit of reverence.
> ~Plato (427 BC-347 BC)

Whenever I get the opportunity to talk with a young adult male about what directions they might take in their life, my advice is always the same. If you want to find and follow the right God, then you should choose a career to pursue that will afford you time for God and family. I strongly advise against any job that will require a lot of traveling, more than five, eight- or nine-hour days a week, and preferably choose an occupation that allows you to work during the same hours your kids are in school.

If you make that your goal, God will help you achieve it. It may not be easy to find a job that affords time for both God and family, but it is also far from impossible. You need to stick to your guns and trust God to help you find it.

Remember the Bible verse that asks what kind of profit is it if you gain the whole world and lose your soul? I wonder what kind of profit it is for a man who gains the whole world while his children lose their souls. Children rarely find their way to such things as honesty, respect, diligence, or God on their own. Therefore, it is extremely important that we forget about such things as better paying jobs with longer hours, and increase responsibility and start concentrating on making our families a priority.

After all, the real God, the One we are hoping to find, is a God of family. In fact, His desire is that we become a part of His family, and He leaves the invitation open for anyone who wants to join. He also cares about human families so much that He has designed rules and procedures for individual family members to follow in order to build a strong, successful, loving family—a family that is unified and God-centered. Like your children, God doesn't care how much money you make. If you trust Him, He will provide for all of your needs and the needs of your family. A simple adage is, if you can't afford it, you don't need it.

WHAT ARE WE TEACHING OUR CHILDREN?

> Train children to live the right way, and when they are old, they will not stray from it.
> ~Proverbs 22:6

I had done numerous odd jobs from the time I was eleven until my sixteenth birthday. As soon as I turned sixteen I got my working papers and almost immediately started a job at a local famous, fast food franchise. It was the early 1970s and, at least this business was all about customer service.

On a Saturday morning shortly after I began working there, they held a mandatory training seminar downstairs at the restaurant. To my surprise, sitting next to the table that held the video projector was a keg of beer. Most of us at the seminar were sixteen years old. I myself had managed to stay away from alcohol until that day and had actually been against the whole idea.

The temptation, however, was more than I was prepared for and once I got used to the taste I ended up making numerous trips to the tap during that two hour presentation. The adults—managers—that were there thought it was cute, I guess, but from that day on I spent most of the next twenty-four years of my life trying to quit drinking.

> Some people get rich by overcharging others, but their wealth will be given to those who are kind to the poor.
> ~Proverbs 28:8

When I was twenty, I worked for a construction company that hired me on as a carpenter's helper. What that meant in reality was a construction laborer. We stripped roofs of their old shingles, dug ditches, stripped paint and demoed old walls, but rarely did any carpenter helping.

On one particular job, which was the total rehab of an old mansion into the corporate headquarters for a large international company, a fellow laborer and myself were told to go downstairs in this old mansion and hide in a huge walk-in safe that was located deep inside the basement. Our job was to hide there for hours until there was some real labor for us to do. The reason was because the construction company I worked for was charging the corporation, who was their customer, for our labor hours. If they sent us home, they could not charge for our time. So, they had us hide on the job and charged a huge rate for our time since we were "carpenters helpers." Consequently, on Christmas Eve that year my boss held a drunken employee party at his house and gave each employee a large bottle of Scotch for Christmas. Seven days later, on New Year's Eve, he laid most of us off. It didn't take long to see the need for the Scotch.

Again, I ask the question, what was the company I was working for training me to be? I went on to have dozens and dozens of customers of my own over the years, and hired as many as eight or nine employees at a time. When God was not my God, you can imagine the type of tactics I may have employed based on my earlier business education.

The goal of any employer should be to point their young employees toward the real God, not the god of money or the god of excessive work. Business owners should display their honesty by treating *their* employers (their customers) with the utmost respect. That means giving them a quality job for an honest price while paying their employees fairly.

The real God wants employers and employees to become people of integrity and high moral excellence. God doesn't want employers to be lowlife robbers who fleece unsuspecting customers and work their employees to death like an old, half-crippled horse, and He doesn't want employees to be worthless sluggards who aren't willing to give an honest day's work for an honest day's pay.

The god of money and the god of excessive work will offer you great things and make extravagant promises, but in the end it will seem to you like "he who earns wages, earns wages to put into a bag with holes" (Haggai 1:6).

The real God will treat you far better than that. It

should be plain to see, given all of the evidence, that making money or work your god is not the right choice.

> All sects are different, because they come from men; morality is everywhere the same, because it comes from God.
> ~Voltaire (1694-1778)

THE PRIDE OF LIFE

> Humility, the place of entire dependence on God, is the first duty and the highest virtue of the creature, and the root of every virtue. And so pride, or the loss of this humility, is the root of every sin and evil.
> ~Andrew Murray, *Humility* (1828-1917)

I don't know if it's like this anymore, but years ago, everyone knew the saying "pride goes before a fall" and quoted it freely on a regular basis. No matter where you were or what you were doing, if you said something prideful or acted with any semblance of pride, someone would let you hear about it. In the circles I travel today, you still hear it ringing out quite frequently, but since pride is encouraged more and more in the education system of today, I doubt it's as common as it once was.

Pride is the thing that convinces a person who says, "We can become our own god," that they are right—that each one of us can be a god. We talked about this earlier, but what a ridiculous, prideful thought it is that we could match wits with the creator of the universe. Orhan Pamak wrote, "There's a lot of pride involved in my refusal to believe in god." And that's so true of many. It's much easier for some to believe that they can be a god, rather than trust and believe in the real God.

One of the hardest things for me to do—and it took many years to get to that place—was to finally say to God, "God, I've tried to do it my way all my life, and failed ... now I am ready to do it Your way." Pride had always stood in my way. I had never been able to achieve the things that mattered to me the most: peace, contentment, joy, and lasting success. But I was not willing to give up on the fight that would prove I could find success on my own. The trouble was, victory never came. And it never would, as long as I let pride stand between me and God.

Pride is a huge blockade that stands between all of us and God. And it is very difficult to tear down.

There are a lot of funny pride stories, fables, and proverbs out there that help open the eyes to see how damaging pride can be. One that always brings a smile to my face and at the same time helps to emphasize this point—that we may have a little trouble bending our will—concerns a Navy ship captain who received a radio message that he would have to divert his ship's course fifteen degrees to the south in order to avoid collision. The Captain radioed back, "Recommend you divert your course fifteen degrees to the north."

"Negative," came the reply. "You will have to divert your course fifteen degrees to the south in order to avoid collision."

Now incensed, the Captain replied, "This is the Captain of a US Navy Ship. I say again, divert your course."

The answer came quickly. "No! I say again, you divert YOUR course!"

At this, the Captain decided to let him know who was boss. He barked, "This is the second largest aircraft carrier in the United Stated Atlantic Fleet. We are accompanied by three destroyers, three cruisers, and numerous support vessels. I demand that you change your course fifteen degrees north—I say again, that's one, five degrees north—or counter-measures will be undertaken to ensure the safety of this ship."

The radio operator's reply? "Well ... okay. We're only a lighthouse, so it's your call.

We can be equally stubborn when it comes to diverting *our* course a little in order to avoid a collision with God. Those who say, "We don't need God," are in essence trying to become the "captain" of their own soul. They can pretend that they will become their own god and say, "I can do it on my own, my own way, and I do not need any assistance from God. God will have nothing to do with my success. It will be all because of me and my awesome ability."

Hmm. ... See? I'm tempted to yell out, "Pride goes before a fall." This type of attitude is on a collision course with the God who created the universe. And it's gonna happen.

Anyway, any vain attempt I've ever made at taking over as master of the universe has always ended up as an ill-fated debacle. There is not one case in all of human history where this perspective has not led to some form of embarrassing ruination. It may take a day, or several years, but it's coming.

The only way out is to change course. A battle of wills with God is a battle you'll lose. Technically, it's already lost before it begins. God is solid, like the lighthouse. He is not going to be willing to budge on this at all. We have got to be willing to submit to His will if we are ever going to have any part in His plans for us.

Consequently, if we are to die to self, we have got to come to the point where we can say with humility, "He is God, and I'm not." We need to be willing to give

Him the credit for all the good in our lives and trust Him with our future—all the success as well as all the failure. If we succeed, it's His doing; if we fail, it's His will. Either way, it's always His call and it's always for our own good. That's His promise if we submit our will and our trust to Him. We must put our faith in Him and allow Him to lead us where He will.

> It is better to be poor and innocent than to be rich and wicked.
> ~Proverbs 28:6

Obviously, after reading about the destruction that worshiping money, work, and immorality can bring upon a family, it should become clear that these things are the exact opposite of the God you should choose to follow.

Anyone who has given any serious thought to finding and following God should at this point know that the real God is a God of love and as such, would not be found in the direction of chaos, immorality, lust, greed, disharmony, disunity, disloyalty, or pride. His desire is for us to live lives that are characterized by love, loyalty, peace, harmony, unity, humility, compassion, and mercy. These are the kind of things that seekers of the true God should be aspiring to find in the God they will decide to choose.

Chapter Twelve

JUDAISM

*T*echnically, you can trace the beginning of Judaism as a religion to the instance when Moses met with God on Mount Sinai and was given the Law. Practically, Judaism dates back nearly 4,000 years to the time of the Bible patriarch Abram, whose name was eventually changed by God to Abraham. Historically, you can trace Judaism's history back through genealogies almost another 2,000 years beyond Abraham to the dawn of time.

There are roughly 14 million followers of Judaism, commonly known as Jews. That is an impressive number, seeing as their heritage and their ancestry can be traced back to one man. There have been converts to Judaism from other nations over the years, but for the most part, most followers, even today, are descendents of Abraham.

Judaism today can be broken down into seven or more distinct groups. At least one group, Secular Judaism, permits the belief that either there is no god, or you can't be sure if there's a god. Other main distinctions are Zionism, Orthodox Judaism, Reform Judaism, Conservative Judaism, Reconstructionist Judaism and Hasidic Judaism.

Judaism, of course, began with the writings of Moses after the children of Israel escaped from their slavery in Egypt. These writings comprise the first five books of both the Jewish and the Christian Bibles and are commonly known as the Law. It is believed that these five books were written by Moses under the inspiration of God Himself. In fact, this is true of the entire Jewish Bible from Genesis to Malachi.

The Jewish Bible traces the steps of mankind from Adam to Abraham and eventually Moses. As I mentioned in the last chapter, the Jewish Bible and the Islamic Qur'an cannot both be correct. In the year 1312 BC, God revealed Himself to the entire nation of Israel—men, women, and children—at Mount Sinai. He announced Himself as the LORD and made a covenant with Moses that the Israelites were His chosen nation and, as such, would be the ones to share the teachings and blessings of God with the rest of the whole world.

Moses and the Israelites were direct descendents of Abraham and Isaac through Jacob. God made a promise to Abraham after Abraham's wife, Sarah, had said to him, "Throw out this slave woman and her son"— referring to Ishmael and his mother (Genesis 21:10). God said, "Don't be troubled about the boy (Ishmael). The descendants I promised you will be from Isaac" (Genesis 21:12), and to the slave woman: "Do whatever Sarah tells you." Later, He instructed Abraham, "Take your *only* son, Isaac, the son you love, and go to the land of Moriah" (Genesis 22:2). Furthermore, God had already said, "Ishmael will be like a wild donkey. He will be against everyone, and everyone will be against him. He will attack all his brothers" (Genesis 16:12).

The promise (mentioned above) that God was talking about here was His promise to give Abraham more descendents than he could count. God said, "I will make you a great nation, and I will bless you. I will make you famous, and you will be a blessing to others. I will bless those who bless you, and I will place a curse on those who harm you. And all the people on earth will be blessed through you" (Genesis 12:2-3). While meeting with Moses and the 3 million people of the nation of Israel at Mount Sinai in 1312 BC, God confirmed that they (the Israelites) were in fact the people he was talking about with Abraham nearly 2,000 years prior.

The writer of the Qur'an, 1,944 years later, wrote that God had told Abraham that Ishmael, his other son, was the child of promise, and that *his* descendents would be the chosen nation. Several times throughout the Bible, however, it is reaffirmed that Israel, who was Isaac's son, Jacob, was in fact the lineage God chose.

Obviously then, both of these accounts cannot be true. Just like there can only be one God, there can only be one chosen nation, if this is what God said.

Since the Biblical account is written 1,944 years prior to the Qur'an account, and since both accounts are virtually the exact opposite, by the rules of historic acceptance alone, there can be no question as to which one is the accurate account.

Unfortunately for biblical Judaism, the story ends with Israel waiting for its promised Deliverer. This Deliverer was known as the Messiah, or Savior, who is the Holy One of God, who would come and deliver mankind from the grip of sin and eternal death.

Since God is holy (pure and without sin) and mankind is not, God had incorporated a system of sacrifices that the people of Israel could make in payment for their sin in order to be temporarily reconciled with Him. There were a variety of sacrifices that could be made for the individual people throughout the year, and then one each year, a special sacrifice, that the high priest would make on behalf of the people that would atone for the sins of the entire nation. When the Deliverer came, He would make a final sacrifice that would pay for the sins of all people who put their trust in His sacrifice, which would be once for all time.

For modern Judaism, they are still waiting for this promised One to come, and since 70 AD, when the last Temple was destroyed, there has been no biblical sacrificial system in place to make atonement for their sin. Many Jews today have come to believe that a blood sacrifice is not necessarily required for their sin. To substantiate this, they cite a verse in Leviticus that states if a person is too poor to offer an animal, they can offer four liters of flour instead.

This, of course, is for individual sins and does not account for the sins of the people for the entire year that the high priest's animal blood sacrifice on the yearly Day of Atonement was designed for. Because of this, many Jews practice a ritual of sin transference on the night before Yom Kipper (The Day Of Atonement) by placing their hands on the head of a chicken and then sacrificing it.

This, although still not biblical, does demonstrate the understanding of at least some Jews that, without a substitutable payment for their sin, they will have to eventually pay for it with their own death.

That is the exact biblical principle that God was trying to demonstrate to the Jewish people all along, by promising a Savior who would come to suffer and die for their sin. He pointed out their sinful nature through the giving of the Law. The Law revealed their sin to them by declaring what actions were considered wrong in God's eyes. He then offered them yearly, temporary forgiveness of their now-exposed sin, which would get them through this life. But, in order to be able to live with God throughout eternity, a special, final, once-for-all sacrifice would have to be made by God's Chosen One (Messiah) that would atone (pay) for all of a person's sin, both past and future. By accepting the Savior's substitutable payment for their sin, that person would be made right with God throughout eternity. And that is why Judaism is still today anxiously waiting for this Savior to come.

If the story ended at Malachi, the God of the Jewish Bible would still be the best candidate of all of the gods and religions that we have looked at so far. All of the accounts of this Jewish Bible are considered by historians, as well as all historical standards, to be accepted historical fact.

These accounts make this God the creator of the entire universe and the giver of all life. There is no other god that can claim this, and no other god was ever before Him. That is why many people joined the Israelites when they became a nation. This God brought Abraham, a direct descendent (eleventh generation) of Noah, out of southern Iraq (Ur) and led him to what is now known as the Holy Land. He promised Abraham innumerable descendants, even though Abraham still had no children at the age of eighty-five.

He is also the God who came and visited Abraham when he was ninety-nine years old and told him that he and his wife, Sarah (age ninety), would have a son. When Abraham tried to persuade God to use Ishmael as the son of promise, God said, "No, Sarah your wife will have a son, and you will name him Isaac. I will make my agreement with him to be an agreement that continues forever with all his descendants" (Genesis 19:17).

This is the God who kept Abraham's descendents alive and caused them to prosper while living as slaves in Egypt. He led them out of slavery in Egypt, sustained them in the desert for forty years, and brought them safely into the Promised Land. He is also the God who has kept the Israelites alive until this day, even though enemies all around the world have been trying to annihilate them for the past 3,324 years.

In all of history, there is clearly no god like this God. As I mentioned, if the story stopped at Malachi, then this would definitely be a God worth considering as you try to decide, *Which God should I choose?*

Chapter Thirteen

CHRISTIANITY

Christianity is the largest religion in the world with an estimated 2.3 billion followers, which constitutes about 32 percent of the world's population. Although Christianity is not growing as fast as other large religions, it does maintain a steady growth rate at roughly the same rate as population growth.

The number of estimated followers of this religion is beyond staggering when you consider that it all started with just one Man who only had three years of His life to devote to ministry, and eleven original followers.

Unfortunately, even though 2.3 billion people say they are Christians, this number can be a little misleading.

Believers in Christ were first called Christians (followers of Christ) at a place called Antioch, which was located in what is today known as southern Turkey. These people were given this name because they acted like devoted followers, or imitators, of Christ. In order to be true followers of Christ, they had to learn and follow His teachings with conviction.

Today, the meaning of the word Christian has a slightly looser definition than it did in the mid-first century. Using America as an indicator, 80 percent of

Americans polled say they are Christians.[66] Of that number (80 percent of 272,274,274 Americans), only 60 million say they attend church regularly. Of that number, less than 12 million profess to read the Bible daily. That's less than 5 percent of all Americans. If America is on average with the rest of the world's Christian statistics, then that 2.3 billion number dwindles down to 1,166,500 people actually following Christ close enough to be recognized as Christians. And that's if people are watching. That number may grow smaller yet when God is doing the counting.

A true indicator of a devoted follower of Christ is their desire to learn daily from God's Word. If you ask a devoted follower, they will tell you that the number one way they learn about Christ's teachings is through His Word.

Christians believe that the Bible, both the Jewish Bible that ended at Malachi (the Old Testament) and the continuation of that book (the New Testament) is the complete, inspired Word of God, and that it is written through and for Christ.

Christians further believe that the promised deliverer (the Messiah) of the Old Testament actually came to earth in the person of Christ. In so doing, He fulfilled at least 108 (and perhaps as many as 300) prophesies that were written about His coming in the Old Testament.

A prophesy in the Bible is similar to a prediction, but more like a foretelling because God told His prophets what *would* happen. It was not a guess.

Some of these prophecies are less than amazing, such as, "This happened to bring about what the Lord had said through the prophet: 'I called my son out of Egypt'" (Mathew 2:15) or, "He will be called a Nazarene" (Mathew 2:23).

When Jesus was born, he was quickly taken by his

Christianity

parents to Egypt from Bethlehem in order to escape the slaughter of all male children in that town two years old and under, ordered by King Herod in an attempt to kill Jesus. After Herod died, God had Jesus' family move to Nazareth, where He was raised. So, He was called out of Egypt, and called a Nazarene.

Other prophesies, much more than amazing, could just plain not happen without God's intervention, like, "The Lord himself will give you a sign: The virgin will be pregnant. She will have a son, and she will name him Emmanuel" (Isaiah 7:14) and, "Then the blind people will see again, and the deaf will hear. Crippled people will jump like deer, and those who can't talk now will shout with joy" (Isaiah 35:5-6).

The Bible states that Mary was the virgin spoken about in Isaiah, chapter seven, nearly 700 years before she was even born. The physical body of Jesus Christ appeared in Mary's womb in a supernatural way. Mary conceived according to a plan designed by God that would not allow sin to enter Christ's flesh. God's own Spirit dwelt in that holy and sinless body of Christ. "God was pleased for all of Himself to live in Christ" (Colossians 1:19). The Bible teaches that Christ was God in human flesh; Immanuel, God with us. Not *a* god, but the very God of heaven Himself. Mary was the virgin girl that God chose for the task of being a vessel to carry the baby Jesus into the world through a normal childbirth, and then raise Him as her own. He chose Joseph to be Jesus' caregiver stepfather who incidentally along with Mary was a descendant of King David (another prophesy).

The reason God chose this approach was because, in order for Jesus to be the substitutable payment for all mankind's sin, He would have to be holy himself and without sin. If He had been conceived in the natural way, with a human father, He would inherit the sin nature that is in all of us, that we originally contracted from the union of Adam and Eve. The sin that Adam and Eve absorbed into their existence by eating the forbidden fruit has been spread from them to all mankind that has lived after them. Because of this, everyone born since then has inherited that sin nature that was first transmitted from Adam and Eve to their children. Our faith in the sacrificial death of Jesus, the sinless God Man, sets our soul and spirit free from this physical body of death that we now live in.

Up until about thirty-five years ago, this whole idea of a woman having a baby without going through the natural processes would have seemed more like science fiction than reality. In fact, the concept of a virgin birth was considered by many to be foolishness for nearly 2,000 years. However, in 1977, with the performance of the first in vitro fertilization process, it was proven that a woman could have a baby placed in her uterus by unnatural means, have the baby grow there in her womb, and then bring the baby into the world through a natural childbirth.

The birth mother in this relationship is known as a gestational surrogate and may or may not have genetic ties to the baby. Since 1978, there have been over 20,000 babies born using this method, which constitutes placing an already formed microscopic baby in a female's uterus, which then grows independent of the mother's physical gene system.

> He will be great and will be called the Son of the Most High. The Lord God will give him the throne of King David, his ancestor.
> ~Luke 1:32

I mentioned Mary and Joseph being descendants of King David, which is verified in Luke 3:23 and Matthew 1:16, because, according to the Old Testament, the Messiah would be a descendant of David and someday sit on his throne. This is extremely important because, as we learned in the last chapter, the Jews are still waiting for Messiah to come. This presents a great problem for Judaism and all those who believe that the Bible stops at the book of Malachi, because, in 70 AD, when Jerusalem was destroyed by the Roman general Titus, all known Jewish birth records were destroyed as well, with the exception of the genealogies found in Luke, chapter three, and Mathew, chapter one, of the Bible.

That means that the very last known person that can ever fulfill this prophecy is Jesus Christ, because, on top of everything else, He is the all-time, last known legal descendant of King David. Anyone else who claims to be is only guessing or lying. So, since there is absolutely no verifiable proof that anyone who has lived since Jesus Christ is a direct descendent of King David, there is no one else who has lived since Him who could possibly be considered a candidate for the Messiah.

As far as those who lived before Jesus, all of history agrees that no one besides Jesus has held the credentials necessary for such a designation. In fact, the possibility of any one man ever, before or after Jesus, fulfilling just a fraction of the prophecies that Jesus fulfilled by His coming is so unlikely that the odds are greater than any number that actually makes sense.

For just having eight of the less than amazing prophecies happen accidentally in one man's lifetime, the probability, according to Professor Peter Stoner, is one chance in 100,000,000,000,000,000 (pronounced one in 100 quadrillion). This only represents the probability of fulfilling just eight of the 108 prophesies of the coming Messiah that Jesus actually did fulfill. If you figure those eight fulfillments by age thirty-three (less than half a lifetime), as Jesus was when He died on the cross, those odds could easily double. The odds of someone fulfilling half of the 108 prophecies that Jesus fulfilled in His lifetime is one with 157 zeros after it![67] We must remember, though, that these weren't predictions or accidents. God said they would happen, and they did.

When God gave Daniel a prophecy about the Messiah coming 470 years after the command was given to rebuild Jerusalem, it wasn't a guess. Daniel was in Babylon while Jerusalem lay in ruins after being destroyed by King Nebuchadnezzar of the Babylonians. After seventy years in captivity, the Persian king who was now ruler in Babylon gave a command that it was okay for the Israelites to go back and rebuild Jerusalem. When you check the year that the command was actually given and count forward 173,880 days (470 years), you come to the exact day we call Palm Sunday. It was the very day that Jesus rode that donkey into the walled city of Jerusalem as King. It would have been startling enough if it had happened anytime during Jesus' lifetime, but to be the very day ... *that* is truly beyond amazing, and only goes to show that God knows exactly what is going to happen and when.

The point of all of this is that God said in various places throughout the Old Testament that He would send the world a Savior who would save mankind from their sin. He said through His prophets that this Savior would be known by all of the different things that would characterize His life. The odds of even a fraction of these things that God said would take place actually happening in one person's life by chance would be impossible, yet Jesus fulfilled every one of them in His short lifetime.

Christians believe that God is one God who has three distinct parts, or persons. *God the Father*, who is Spirit; He is everywhere at once, knows all things and has ultimate power over all creation. He is the eternal God. *God the Son*, the second part of this Trinity, is Jesus Christ. In the person of Jesus Christ, God took on a sin-free, physical body and dwelt among us. Jesus was God in human flesh. The third part of God is known as *the Holy Spirit*. The Holy Spirit lives inside believers. When a person truly puts their faith in Jesus, it's because they believe that He was God in the flesh and that He came for the purpose of being the only acceptable sacrifice for their life of sin. They furthermore believe that He died paying for that sin on a cross at Calvary and, three days later, that He rose from the dead. When a person truly believes that, God sends His Holy Spirit into that person's body to help live the kind of life He planned for them. This is much like when He placed His Spirit in Jesus, except that in our body, our spirit lives there too. God's Spirit gives us power (to serve God and live for Christ), love, and self control (1 Timothy 1:7).

Our spirit does strive at times with God's Spirit, and that is why it is so vitally important for a Christian to exhaust all efforts to grow in the grace and knowledge of God, through Christ.

Together, these are the three parts of the one eternal God. He is known as the Triune God, or the Trinity, because He has these three specific parts, but it is important to understand that He is one God with three parts, *not* three separate gods.

God raised Jesus from the dead, and if God's Spirit is living in you, he will also give life to your bodies that die. God is the One who raised Christ from the dead, and he will give life through his Spirit that lives in you.
~Romans 8:11

Christians believe that after Jesus died on the cross to pay the penalty that was due for all sins, He was buried in a tomb, and then three days later He miraculously rose from the dead. Because He gave his perfect life as a sacrifice for the imperfect lives that people live, mankind now has a way to have their sin paid for without actually having to pay the price themselves.

When Jesus rose from the dead three days later, He proved that He has power over death, and subsequently power over sin as well. The Bible says that our sin can only be paid for in one of two ways. Either we pay for it ourselves by eternal punishment in hell, or we use the sacrificial death of the perfect life of Jesus Christ to pay for it by asking God to apply it to our life. Once we ask God for that free gift, He completely forgives us of our responsibility for it. He cleanses us of our sin. The Bible says that if we confess with our mouth the Lord Jesus and believe in our hearts that God has raised Him from the dead, we will be saved (Romans 10:9).

Biblical Christianity teaches that when Jesus left here, He went back to heaven to prepare a place for believers, and that He will someday return for them. There is detailed information in the Bible concerning this event, and after weighing all the evidence portrayed it seems clear that we are living in the generation that will experience the return of Christ.

In the meantime, all people who die before this second coming of Christ will go to one of two places—either

Christianity

to be with Christ in heaven, or to hell. Those who go to be with Christ will remain in Christ's presence, at least spiritually, until they are brought back to earth with Christ at His second coming. At that point they will be reunited with their bodies. Their bodies will be remade without the sin nature and their spirits placed back in them. They will no longer experience such things as sin, pain, sorrow, or dying and will be given the great responsibility of ruling and reigning with Christ.

Those who do not believe will be placed in hell to await the final judgment day. On that day they will be cast into the Lake of Fire where they will be doomed to live throughout eternity.

Although this seems like a lot to absorb, as you study through the Bible and experience Christ in your life, it all becomes reality.

> Us Tareyton smokers would rather fight than switch!
> ~James Jordan Jr. (1930-2004)

In an advertising campaign designed to promote loyalty among smokers of a certain brand of cigarette, the slogan "Us Tareyton smokers would rather fight than switch!"[68] became an overwhelming success. The ads featured beautiful models with black eyes, which was supposed to signify that they would rather fight with other smokers than change their brand. The campaign ran in various forms from 1963-1981 and moved Tareyton into the top ten brands of cigarettes sold during the 1960s.

Christianity is among the most persecuted of all religions. At a recent interfaith conference in Hungary, it was reported that persecution leads to the death of 105,000 Christians each year. That equates to one

Christian being killed every five minutes somewhere around the world, simply because of their faith.[68] According to World Evangelical Alliance, over 200 million Christians in at least sixty countries are being persecuted (not to death) yearly for their faith. Of those, it is estimated that over 1 million are children.

A simple solution to this problem would seem to be, just deny your faith, and then the enemies of Christians would leave you alone. Christians, however, would rather die a horrible death at the hands of their enemies than deny their faith in Christ. Unlike Tareyton smokers, they take a slightly different view of their enemies. So different, in fact, that they love them and actually pray for them. In many cases, even while they are being persecuted or put to death.

This controversial attitude toward enemies is not the only odd quirk that sets Christianity apart from all other religions. A normal reaction would be to hate those who hate you, get even with those who wrong you, and lie to save your own skin.

> Protect the truth that you were given; protect it with the help of the Holy Spirit who lives in us.
> ~2 Timothy 1:14

Christians are taught the exact opposite. To love all people, as Christ loves them, to forgive all people, as Christ forgave them, and always tell the truth, even when it causes your demise. These are tough orders and the exact opposite of our default attitudes. It is certain that they are unnatural to us and could only be achieved with God's help.

The Bible teaches that when you put your faith in Christ, God makes you into a new creation. All the old attitudes are transformed into new ones that reflect the attitude of Christ. You become a new person who loves your enemies, trusts God to do the getting even, and tells the truth. As noted, He gives you the power to accomplish this radical change in your human disposition by sending His Spirit to live in you and help out.

In spite of persecution—which sometimes includes great monetary loss, torture, imprisonment and even death—millions of Christians allow themselves to be put through this unfair treatment, which adds great credibility to the source of their faith. After all, why would not just one someone, but millions of "someones," allow themselves to be tortured and put to death just because they won't denounce their God, if their God were not the real God?

It is clear from all of the evidence we have that there is no greater God than the God of the Bible. That is why so many millions are willing to be put to death rather than deny their faith. Since there is no greater God, and even creation itself points to the God of the Bible as its sole Creator, it is clear that this God is the God we should choose.

Chapter Fourteen

CHANGING GOD'S RECIPE

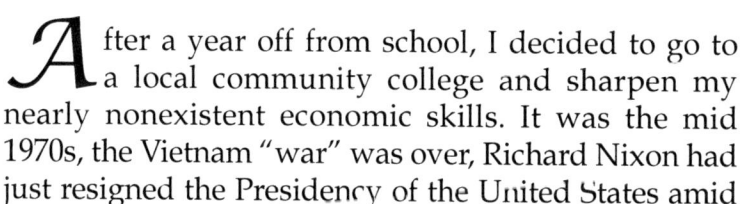

*A*fter a year off from school, I decided to go to a local community college and sharpen my nearly nonexistent economic skills. It was the mid 1970s, the Vietnam "war" was over, Richard Nixon had just resigned the Presidency of the United States amid scandal, and Gerald Ford, who had been appointed Vice President after Spiro Agnew's resignation, had now been appointed President.

You may notice I said *appointed*. Gerald Ford became the only president that no one ever voted for, either as vice president or president. It was a crazy time in history. The hippie-prevalent sixties had given way to a different kind of America in the 1970s. It had literally changed before my very eyes. Drugs were cheap and everywhere, most people I knew were either drunk or stoned most of the time, couples were living together instead of getting married, and divorce, murder, abortion, and riots were on the rise. Pollution was terrible. The crying Indian commercials reminded us that PCB's, DDT, leaded gas, acid rain, nasty smoke stacks, and litter were destroying the environment. Life was turning upside-down from what I remembered as a child just five or six years earlier.

Which God Should I Choose?

I remember riding down the highway toward my college. Long hair, headband, 1964 Ford van, radio blasting. The news came on—which I normally didn't listen to—but I didn't change the station this time because I wasn't really aware it was on. One of my college professors was teaching us to scream really loudly in the morning at the top of our lungs (I can't remember why—some adrenalin exercise, I think). I do know, there I was, going down the road sixty miles an hour, screaming my fool head off, and I didn't notice that the news had started.

When I stopped screaming, I heard the news guy talking about all these awful, depressing things that were happening. As I listened, it was like one bad news story right after another. When he finished, I shut the radio off and started to reflect a little about how messed up society was. I remember wondering, *Is there any way to fix all this?*

As I thought about it—this clueless, nineteen-year-old, second generation hippie—I realized that the only way possible to end this craziness that was going on all around me was if everybody started doing what the Bible said to do. Trust me, I did not know much about the Bible. My father used to drop me off for Sunday School at a less-than-solidly-biblical church, but I learned enough there to know that the opposite of everything that I was seeing falling down around me was in that book. That was the answer.

At that point, I started seeking God. Unfortunately, it was quite a lengthy search. I tried, but my lack of wisdom overtook me. There were a lot of people looking for answers back then, just as there are today. But, people just seemed to complain about the conditions and continue on in the same direction, doing the same things but expecting different results.

I decided to find a Bible-based church. I had been around long enough to know that there were many churches that did not have a proper understanding of the Bible. My intentions were good, but searching for a church without really knowing what I was doing led to yet another disastrous outcome. Before I could find the kind of church I had set out to find, I ended up in a church of the same denomination that my father had dropped me off at as a child. Persuasive circumstances led me to settle in for all the wrong reasons. I gave up my quest for truth and accepted a watered-down version of Christianity.

Before too long, I began to slowly realize that most people there were saying one thing, but doing another: me included. I became disillusioned. I wasn't growing closer to God; I was growing closer to myself. Although I had initially sought to find God, my understanding of Him had not grown very much at all. I began hanging around people that were pulling me in a different direction. Because I had allowed myself to get involved in another half-hearted religion, I eventually gave up on the desires that had drawn me there in the first place, turned my back on God, and rejoined the fallen world. I'm praying that I might be able to help you avoid a lot of the wrong turns I took by giving you the best possible information to help you choose the right direction. I'm suspecting, at least for some, that a similar revelation to the one I had back when I was nineteen may have led you to this book. I was right back then. I just lost sight of it. It would take another twenty years for me to come back around to that understanding. The only answer, now almost forty years later, to correct all of the problems in the world today is if everyone followed the teachings of the Bible with all their heart. Of course, that won't happen.

What does happen, though, is we learn that the Bible is filled with wisdom that we do not have. The Bible says it is the living Word of God. It's hard to understand what that means until you spend time with the Author.

The Bible records the creation of all things. Everything that we know of that has to do with God begins there: God Himself, heaven, hell, the devil, right and wrong, even peace and love. They are all defined there (in the Bible) first. Anyone who starts a movement, cult, or religion using anything that is found in the Bible and twists it or changes it into something else, but uses some or even many of its intricate existing parts, is guilty of evil wrongdoing on a whole bunch of different levels.

Imagine if I start a hamburger franchise and call it by a famous, established name. I have a clown and a famous meal for kids, but I change a lot of the classic ideas that made it famous and ruin its reputation. I use poor-quality ingredients, change the name of the marquis items and fall short of the high standards that the original company has set. I may draw you in with more attractive pricing and dazzling offers, but in the end you are going to get a substandard product, while the real owner of the famous company is not going to be at all happy with your meal.

In the past few chapters we have looked at several cults and religions that have developed out of the roots of the Bible, but have changed the teachings of the Bible to fit their needs or agenda. No matter what, if you change authentic history, by definition you have become a fraud.

Imagine if a teacher in school started teaching that Abraham Lincoln was never president of the United States, but merely a homeless person that snuck in the White House on occasion and impersonated the

Changing God's Recipe

president. This teacher would be considered a nut. You can't take the known truth and change it to meet your own agenda and ever be right. Since the Bible has been accepted as fact by historical standards for nearly 2,000 years, any teaching that deviates from any part of it has got to be a lie.

Therefore, any cult or any religion that links itself to the Bible but alters its teaching should be considered false. If you examine the facts surrounding these cults and religions, you will always find evidence to support this finding, without exception. You can never find the truth while you are following a lie.

As we have seen repeatedly throughout this book, most religions today that have a god started out by taking ingredients unique to the Bible, changed them around, added their own secret ingredients and created their own god, kind of like cooking with somebody else's recipe, but not liking the finished dish the way it is. The question is, why? Why is God's Word not good enough at face value? Why do people feel the need to change it? Left to itself, God's Word is living and powerful. It has the power to change lives. But changed from itself, it becomes powerless — powerless to the hearer anyway. To the leaders who change it, it becomes a powerful source of income. Great riches have been amassed through the misuse and abuse of God's Word.

If you change God's Word around, you can charge people to let the corpses of their loved ones remain in a cemetery. You can charge people to get into heaven. You can charge people to pray their loved ones into heaven. You can charge for healing services and get people to give you their wives, their children, their riches, and property. You can persuade people with promises of future rewards to strap bombs to themselves and blow up people you hate; you can convince people that the more they give you the more God will give them. You can persuade people to serve you and bring in more converts (which means more money) in hopes of receiving a limited place in heaven, and, in certain instances, you can even fool people into believing that you are God.

Beyond the leaders though, why is the original Word of God not good enough for the millions of people who follow a different teaching? After all, in every instance, it costs you more than you can afford to give, and the promises that were made never end up being fulfilled.

The answer is simply this: people do not feel they can trust God's Word as it was written. That it is not reliable ... and why is that?

If you are younger than sixty-five years old, then chances are you were a student after God was removed from public schools in 1962. A Supreme Court decision banned prayer to God in schools that year. At the same time, while not allowing God to be there to defend Himself, the teaching of the theory of evolution began to escalate.

This created a couple of problems for kids. Number one, if the first chapter of the Bible got it wrong, then the rest of the Bible became questionable. Second, if we evolved from pond scum, then we have no true worth. We are not valuable at all, and there is no incentive to do good, because we live by accident and then we die. There is nothing else. We have no purpose for living.

SIMPLE MATH

Through his power all things were made — things in heaven and on earth, things seen and unseen, all powers, authorities, lords, and rulers. All

things were made through Christ and for Christ. He was there before anything was made, and all things continue because of him.
~Colossians 1:16-17

There are three common denominators in all false religions that a person trying to decide which God they should choose must be aware of. When searching for the right God, it will be important to recognize these things when you see them.

DID YOU EVER STOP TO THINK THAT WHEN GOD MADE THE EARTH THE REST OF THE UNIVERSE WAS EMPTY?

The first thread all religions that have sprung from variations of the Bible have in common is not a single one believes Genesis, chapter one, is true. They cannot. Because, if Genesis, chapter one, is correct, then there is a Creator God who created man in His image and for His good pleasure, and every word that follows falls against the next in truth like dominoes in a row fall against each other until the end.

If Genesis, chapter one, is correct, then anyone who changes any word of the chapters that follow is a liar. If people trusted Genesis, chapter one, then they would not follow false teachers, and false religions would die and the gods they have created with them.

Why is it harder to believe that God created the heavens and the earth than it is to believe in evolution? Again, there are a couple of problems. Number one, many people choose to believe evolution no matter how compelling the evidence for God's creation of the earth, because they would rather follow a lie than follow the God of the Bible.

And number two, since the theory of evolution has been engrained in the mind of the average person from childhood, God's Word, as it stands, is not reliable. How can you have billions of years between the first animals and the first humans on one hand, and on the other have animals and humans created in the same week? If you carefully examine the evidence though, it takes a lot more faith to believe in evolution than it does to believe we live in God's creation.

First of all, the theory of evolution is not a theory at all. It is a model. It should be properly called the model of evolution because in order to be a theory it would have to be able to be tested. If a theory is tested and proven true, then it becomes a law. If proposals, suppositions, or models cannot be tested, then they remain models. This means it is impossible to test the model of evolution, so it can never become even a theory, let alone a law.

On the other hand there are several laws, (theories that have been proven), that the model of evolution would have to break in order to be true. The thing about scientific laws though, is that they cannot be broken—laws such as the first law of thermodynamics, which in simple terms states that the amount of matter or energy in the universe cannot change. No more can be created and none can be destroyed. It can only change form.

The second law of thermodynamics states that as matter changes, it always becomes less useable. Its usefulness gradually deteriorates over time. If true (which obviously it is), evolution would break this law, because the model shows species progressing as they evolve and becoming more complex.

According to the laws of science, this cannot happen. So, with what we have, you cannot create something out of nothing. We as humans on the earth cannot do that. It can't happen.

But what does Genesis, chapter one, say? In verse one, it says, "God created the Heavens and the earth." Furthermore, we know from reading the Bible that He created them from nothing. He spoke them into existence. According to our laws, He could not do that, but as God, He has a much higher likelihood of being able to accomplish this task than the model of evolution would have of breaking not one, but every scientific law. As much as every religion that has sprung from using parts of the Bible denies that God created the heavens and the earth, God claims He did, and He is the first known One who ever made such a claim.

As we make our own observations, it is clear that you cannot get order out of disorder. Nothing improves itself by doing nothing. Left alone, everything slowly deteriorates into chaos.

I used to grow a pretty decent garden that was admired and coveted by my neighbors. One year, after I cultivated and planted my garden, I left for the summer. As I headed home just before Labor Day that year, I envisioned a beautiful garden, rich with fall harvest, awaiting my return. Guess what I found instead? The fruitful things I had planted were almost completely choked out by useless, nasty-looking weeds.

From this experience, I can kind of imagine what the earth would look like if there was a big explosion in space that somehow generated life out of rocks (that apparently somehow formed themselves). Since our laws tell us none of this could have happened anyway, it is hard to get my mind completely around it, but even so, it doesn't take much to guess that whatever life would have been formed from such a cataclysmic event would degenerate back into rocks in a very short amount of time.

Another scientific law that defines life as we know it states that matter cannot be created or destroyed in an isolated system. This is called the Scientific Law of Conservation of Matter. It has been argued that we may not live in an isolated (closed) system, but that space may go on and on, thereby letting things in and out. Although that is not likely, it really doesn't matter because the earth itself is a closed system. God said it in Genesis, chapter one, verses six through ten: "Then God said, 'Let there be something to divide the water in two.' So God made the air and placed some of the water above the air and some below it. God named the air 'sky.' Evening passed, and morning came. This was the second day. Then God said, 'Let the water under the sky be gathered together so the dry land will appear.' And it happened. God named the dry land 'earth' and the water that was gathered together 'seas.' God saw that this was good."

There are many interesting statements in Genesis, chapter one, that we will cover, but probably none more striking than verse nine. Verse nine says that God, after creating the waters, gathered them all into one place. Moses, writing as God dictated to him 3,500 years ago, wrote this verse down, not realizing that it would take thousands of years for science to catch up to and verify it.

My niece, who is an environmental engineer for NASA, and in fact nominated this year for engineer of the year, recently told me of a study done on the earth's water supply. The study found that all of the water we have in our environment is the same water we have ever had. No more is being added or created. It is a fixed supply that cannot grow. It cycles over and over and no water is ever added nor naturally lost. This study tells us that whenever water was created, it was all created at once, and all gathered together within the earth's atmosphere and designed as part of a system that would cycle continuously.

The model of evolution states that there was an explosion in the universe somewhere that threw things randomly throughout space and eventually fell into order, while Genesis 1:9 tells us that God gathered the waters He created into one place. Only one of these statements can be true.

If my niece's study is correct, it would be some trick for a mammoth explosion in space to throw all of the water that was created in that explosion to this one little planet, out of millions, and then have that fixed amount of water trapped in an environment where it would continue to cycle for billions of years (by accident). Oddly, this would break yet another scientific law, because nothing gains order on its own. Order cannot be obtained out of chaos.

As you read down through Genesis, chapter one, a recurring statement you find is "after its kind." Today, we call this the scientific Law of Biogenesis. Even though God said it, nobody could really prove it until about 5,800 years after it was said. In the year 1864, a man named Louis Pasteur (who we get the term "pasteurize" from) performed a series of experiments that demonstrated life could only arise from existing life.

He found that the production of new, living things could only come from other living things, and more importantly, only by reproduction (e.g., chickens lay eggs that hatch and develop into chickens, and monkeys have babies that develop into monkeys). Furthermore, life does not arise from nonliving material. Pasteur summarized his findings by saying "*Omne vivum ex vivo*," which is Latin for "all life is from life."

Up until the time of Louis Pasteur's findings, there

was speculation among some, of life arising from nonliving things through spontaneous generation. Spontaneous generation supposes that life can be created without seeds, eggs, or parents.

The creating of life from nonliving material is known as abiogenesis. Scientists who believe there was such a thing once, say that the conditions required for abiogenesis no longer exist. Concerning life coming from nonliving things through spontaneous generation, Pasteur stated, *"La génération spontanée est une chimère"* (Spontaneous generation is a dream.).[70]

Another interesting statement in Genesis chapter one is that God created the sun, moon and stars to be light for the earth. Genesis 1:14-19 says, "Then God said, 'Let there be lights in the sky to separate day from night. These lights will be used for signs, seasons, days, and years. They will be in the sky to give light to the earth.' And it happened. So God made the two large lights. He made the brighter light to rule the day and made the smaller light to rule the night. He also made the stars. God put all these in the sky to shine on the earth, to rule over the day and over the night, and to separate the light from the darkness. God saw that all these things were good. Evening passed, and morning came. This was the fourth day."

The model of evolution states that there was a huge explosion that created the stars in the universe, our sun being one of them, around 4.54 billion years ago. The problem is, at the speed of light, light from the farthest known galaxy, which is 13.5 billion light years away, would not reach us for another 9 billion years, yet we found it because we can see it. The only way possible for us to see light from stars that has not traveled far enough in their lifetime to reach us is if they were created with their light already shining here. It is easier for me to believe that God created the stars around 6,000 years ago with their lights shining here already so we could see them then it is for me to believe that we can see the light from stars that will not reach us for another 9 billion years yet. What kind of sense does that make?

It wouldn't matter if the earth was 4.5 billion years old (evolution) or 6,000 years old (Bible). We would not be able to see the light. The whole "billions of years" model is a total farce with odds so large that there is not a number big enough to give it.

This should tell us that, if the only way the universe could have come into existence is if it happened all at once, just the way that God says it did, and, every god, religion and cult there is denies that, then God is the true God and all other gods, religions, and cults are false. That should also be a scientific law itself, if it is not one already.

Someone has said that if you had one million monkeys typing continuously on one million typewriters, the odds of one of them to accidentally typing "In the beginning God created the Heavens and the earth" would be one in 120 with sixty zeros after it. That number is so big that it is not comprehensible.

The second thread that all false religions have in common is not one believes that John, chapter one, is true. No other religion save Christianity recognizes Jesus Christ as Savior and Lord. The Bible teaches that Jesus is the very God of Heaven. He left His place there and allowed Himself to be born on the earth in order to suffer for the sins of all mankind by being crucified on a cross, but He is relegated by all other religions to be either a prophet, good teacher, or just another god. They simply do not believe that He is who He says He is.

> I am busily engaged in the study of the Bible. I believe it is God's word because it finds me where I am. ... I believe the Bible is the best gift God has ever given to man. All the good of the Savior of the world is communicated to us through the Book.
> ~Abraham Lincoln, Sixteenth President of the United States (1809-1865)

The third thread, or common denominator, of all false religions is that they distort the original accepted Word of God.

You have probably played the game where you whisper a message in someone's ear and then they in turn whisper it to the person next to them. When the message has gone around the whole room, the last person recites it to the original message-teller to see if it is the same message.

As the message goes from ear to ear around the room, something funny happens. By the time the message gets to the last person, it hardly resembles the original message at all. People in the middle of the room, who were responsible for some of the message's major shifts, look at one another and shamefully shrug their shoulders. Everyone tries to make excuses as to how they came up with what they said. Sometimes it's because the message wasn't relayed correctly, sometimes it's because it wasn't heard or interpreted correctly, and sometimes it's because an individual decides to change it to how they think it should go. If you want to know what the true, original message was, you have to go back to the original teller of the message.

There are a lot of reasons for how badly the true, original message gets messed up, and the more people there are, and the more time that goes by, the further the message gets from the original.

That is much the same as it is with God's Word. God decided who would write down His Word, what would be included in it, and how it would be accomplished. Once it was completed, that was the true, original, complete message. In some cases, without copies of the message, it would spread by word of mouth—and we already know how that goes. In other cases, those who did have copies decided to change the message a little (or a lot) to how they thought it should be told.

The outcome is always the same. When the message is declared, either it doesn't resemble the true, original message in the least, or possibly it is similar with only subtle variations. Either way, when you go back and check the original, true message, you find that it has been distorted.

Many variations, replacements, and even additions to the original written Word of God have materialized over the years. Some as books which would include Islam's Qur'an (653-656 AD), the Sikhs' Adi Granth, given in 1708 AD, or the Mormon's Book of Mormon, written in 1830 AD. Others were transmitted through traditions, fables, and legends. Whatever the media, when you go back and compare these other messages to God's original message (which today we call the Bible), you can see how distorted the truth has become as it strays from God's Word.

If we truly want to know more about God and are going to take the time to read about Him and try to determine His desires for us, wouldn't it make the most sense to go back to the original, recorded, accepted message from God to get our factual information, rather than trust someone who somewhere along the line has taken the original message and changed it into their own words to meet their own needs?

THE QUESTION THEN BECOMES, "BUT HOW DO WE KNOW THAT THE BIBLE IS THE TRUE WORD OF GOD?"

WHO AM I ... WHY AM I HERE?

If you are coming to the place where you realize there must be a God because all of the amazing things in this life could not just happen by chance, then you are on the verge of discovering that you (who you really are) have true worth. You're not an accident that happened millions of years after a pollywog crawled up on shore and became a monkey. You're a calculated choice made by the same God who created the universe and everything else that is in it. You are worth something. In fact, God says that you are worth so much to Him that He gave His only Son as a sacrifice for you. I do not pretend to know God's ways or plans, but I do know this: He created you for a purpose. Ephesians 2:10 says, "God has made us what we are. In Christ Jesus, God made us to do good works, which God planned in advance for us to live our lives doing." God has had a plan for you all along and has been patiently waiting for you to come to that understanding.

One of the things that interests me most is that God decided when each one of us would be born (the hour, day, week, month, and year). So, I could have been born 300 years ago when they were pulling teeth without novocaine, or 800 years ago when they still thought the world was sitting on the back of a turtle. I kind of wish God had waited fifteen more years for me, so I could have avoided the dentist I had when I was a kid, and the family doctor for that matter. Both of them were cut from the same cloth, as I recall. They were both needle happy. Plus I'd be fifteen years younger. But God had a plan for my life that meant I had to be born at the moment I was. And that goes for you too. His plan for your life required you to be born when you were. As I look back through my life, and even look into the comings and goings of my recent and distant ancestors, I can see the miraculous methods God used to steer me toward where I am now.

God not only planned for the very minute you would be born, but He also planned for the exact family and location. You could just have easily been born to a Jewish family in Nazi Germany or an idol-worshiping family in the land of Canaan that burned their children as sacrifices. You may be thinking, *That might have been better*, but trust me—when you figure out why you're here, you will thank God for the time period you were born, the family you were born to, and the nation you were born in.

Wouldn't it be neat to start recognizing why God had you born when and where He did? God told the prophet Jeremiah, "Before I made you in your mother's womb, I chose you. Before you were born, I set you apart for a special work. I appointed you as a prophet to the nations" (Jeremiah 1:5). Considering what Jeremiah had to go through later on in life, if it were me, I may have been tempted to say sarcastically, "Thanks a lot, Lord," but Jeremiah, even though he is known as the weeping prophet, never blinked.

Because he told King Jehoiakim and the people of Judah the things God told him to concerning God's coming judgment, he was mocked, persecuted, and thrown into prison. After his release, as the Babylonian army surrounded Jerusalem, God told Jeremiah to tell the people that anyone who left the city and surrendered to Nebuchadnezzar would live, but anyone who stayed in the walled city would die. The king's officers were so infuriated by this talk that they took Jeremiah and put him down a well that had only mud left in it. They left him there to starve and die. God did send a man to help him escape, and within the next few years, Jeremiah saw what the Talmud describes as millions of his fellow countrymen either killed or taken captive by the Babylonians. Jeremiah, however, was spared, set free by his Babylonian captors, allowed to stay in Jerusalem, and could come and go as he pleased.

Just like Jeremiah, the real God has a plan and purpose for your life as well. None of this means anything, however, if you don't choose the right God.

Chapter Fifteen

ON THE ROCKS

*F*or me, anything that I leave to chance is going to end up in turmoil. It doesn't matter if it's something as simple as my lawn or as complicated as my computer—without planning and intervention, anything I leave to its own will always deteriorate into chaos. If I do not care for my lawn (which someone has had to have made into a lawn in the first place)—mowing it regularly, clearing off fallen branches, repairing damaged areas, weeding, and so forth—before long it will be a field of brush. Similarly, if I do not maintain my computer (which didn't make itself) by keeping it organized and free of viruses, soon it would not work properly, if at all.

So how can we imagine that this world came into being on its own, organized itself, and maintains itself? It doesn't matter how far back in time you go, whether it's thousands of years or billions of years, at some point in history, somebody, somewhere, had to create something out of nothing.

Some say that billions of years ago there was an explosion that formed the universe. That's all well and good, but where did the materials come from that caused the explosion? And, if there weren't big rocks already that exploded into smaller rocks to make planets, then how did the explosion of gases make rocks? And where did the gases come from?

As you look out across the sky, it's ridiculous to think that whatever is out there has always been there, forever and ever, and that it never had a beginning—or, if it did have a beginning, that it formed out of absolutely nothing on its own. It is, however, not so ridiculous to think that someone, somewhere, had to initially make something.

When you get beyond the idea of the universe, stars, and planets, what about life? Who started that? Did pond scum, which formed out of nothing, grow amoebas that eventually turned into frogs that hopped up onto land and became monkeys? Did these monkeys turn into humans, horses, and hyenas over time?

Life is interesting, and far more complicated to make, I would imagine, than rocks. We don't understand everything completely that there is to know about life (and by "we," I mean what humans have discovered). We have figured out a few things that we didn't know 150 years ago when someone suggested that mankind evolved from pollywogs. What we now know is that all species, whether animal or human, are each constructed differently according to the DNA information they receive from their parents. Although DNA talk is complicated and boring to most, it can be summarized by saying that there is a library's worth of encoded information within each cell in your body, whether you're a human or a hippo, that tells exactly how your body is going to be constructed. It is extremely close to your parents and ancestors. There are more bits of information in one percent of the cells in your body than 315 times the number of grains of sand on the earth. The information is genius and perfectly read into the construction of your body.

What it says is what is built. The errors in your body are from the information given by your parents, not from errors in reading and building you from that blueprint of written information.[71]

The point for us who are trying to choose the right God is that somewhere, at sometime, somebody had to write that code of intensely detailed instructions. I call it a code because it's not written in English. It's probably not really a code at all, but written in somebody's own language — I'm guessing God's. It's easily readable if you have the key, because the little motor that takes the information and puts a body together one cell at a time in its mother's womb understands it completely.

I have heard that if the information in one cell was written in a continuous line, it would stretch to the moon and back more than once, and it doesn't matter if it is the cell of a paramecium or a pterodactyl. In every living thing, the information for their structure is given to them by their parents. So, a blowfly cannot become a blowfish, and a monkey cannot become a man. The little motor that reads the information and puts the body together comes from the parents as well, so it can never change into something else. Every living thing has to be replicated after its own kind.

There are, of course, several species that prove beyond a doubt that one species cannot slowly change to another. My favorite to discuss is the giraffe. A male giraffe can grow to be twenty-five feet tall. That creates a long distance between his heart and his brain. In order to pump blood up his eight foot long neck to his brain, it requires him to have a huge heart. Giraffe hearts can weigh over twenty-five pounds and be over two feet long. Their blood pressure is about triple that of a human being.

Because of that, a couple of things in their bodies

had to be adjusted. For one, they have to have very thick artery walls in their limbs to handle the high blood pressure, as well as thick skin and tissue to prevent leaks. This all sounds normal and proportionate to its size, I know. The trick comes in when it bends over for a drink of water, because without somebody figuring it out ahead of time, its huge heart would now be pumping blood downhill to its brain at three times the blood pressure of you and me. Its parents, however, in their DNA, had a provision for a system of regulating valves in its neck which restricts the flow of blood to its brain when it bends over for a drink. At the same time, its system stores an exact amount of blood needed at its brain, so that when it stands up quickly, there is enough blood already there while the valves are opening back up and the required flow rate is being restored. No other species has that. No other mom and dad could have given it that. It could only have come from giraffe parents, and giraffe parents don't grow on trees, or in ponds. Giraffes had to start out with two giraffes, a male and a female, already created. There's absolutely no other way to explain it.

Therefore, it is axiomatic that at the beginning of each species, whether it's a giraffe or a gerbil, there had to be a male and a female that were created with this library of information written in their DNA (with the little motor included) that reads the instructions and assembles everything together as written, in order to pass it on to their offspring.

This narrows the field dramatically as we sift through the many gods and goddesses that are prevalent in the world today. We can automatically cancel out any that do not understand creation.

By not understanding creation, I mean that they (and their followers who made them up) don't understand that gases can't form themselves out of nothing and then explode or get hit by lightning to form matter, and matter, once formed, cannot evolve into life. They don't understand that even the simplest life forms are extremely complicated and come with extensive written instructions for every single offspring they propagate. If they don't understand even the simplest rules of nature—that stuff doesn't just appear out of nothing, and order never arises out of chaos—they cannot be God.

Therefore, it is not unreasonable to conclude as we try to decide which God we should choose, that we settle on a God that not only has the power and ability to make inanimate things like gas, rocks, and stars out of nothing, but also the has ability to make living things like people, plants, and animals with blueprints of building instructions built into each cell that boggle the mind. This is the kind of God we should be looking for. This is the kind of God we should choose. After all, why would we choose a god that doesn't do anything, when we can be certain that there is a real God who does? The real God would have had to be involved in the creation of the universe and all that is in it. Anyway, *someone* had to be. Someone had to make the nonliving things as well as the living things, and if not God, then who?

In the past several chapters, we have examined the existing facts surrounding many of the plethoras of gods that are available to choose from. Many of the characteristics of the false gods in the world today are similar, and so the ones we reviewed may be a representation of more than just the ones mentioned.

Only one God has no other god even remotely similar, and so the evidence should point to that God as being unique and superior in all of His ways. You should be able to determine by the evidence given that there really is only one true God that we should consider choosing, and He is the only one who is right for us.

As we sift through these many gods available, and it becomes clear that there are subtle similarities among all of them but one, the choice process becomes that much simpler. Only one demonstrates His incomparable and awesome power throughout history, toward all mankind.

In fact, you should be able to determine by the evidence that either He is the right God because all of the facts prove that He is, or else you should be able to determine by the evidence that all of the other gods are not the right god because all of the facts prove that they are not.

IF ANYBODY NEEDED MORE PROOF

Judaism, which began at the time of Moses, was populated by a group of people who could trace their heritage back to both the beginning of time and, ultimately, to God, because of the writings of Moses. Moses demonstrated that in his writings—at least statistically—he could only have known about the things he recorded if God showed him what to write. Professor Peter Stoner estimates that the statistical probability of Moses writing down the thirteen events in Genesis, chapter one, both accurately and in order, without God's help—and so, by accident—is one chance in 31,135,104,000,000,000,000,000 (1 in 31 x 10^{21}).[72] That is a number (thirty-one octillion or 31,000 quadrillion) that cannot be understood except with the help of an object lesson.

This is just an estimate, but if you covered the entire United States two feet deep in quarters, put a mark on one of the 31,000 quadrillion quarters, and then blindfolded a person and sent them into the United States to pick up one quarter, they would have the same chance of picking up the one marked quarter as Moses would have had of accidentally writing down the thirteen events in Genesis, chapter one, both accurately and in order.

The leaders of Judaism determined from these writings and other Old Testament scripture that there were also four things that *only* the Messiah could perform, and that this would prove that He was the One whom God had sent. They were: one, to give sight to a person blind from birth; two, to cast out a mute demon; three, to raise a person from the dead after being dead for four days; and four, to heal a person with leprosy.

As you read through the Bible, you will see that Jesus fulfilled these four things, as well as at least 108 other predictions foretold hundreds and even thousands of years before He came. Statistically, the chance of anyone doing this apart from God's intervention defies all logic and human comprehension. You'd probably have to cover the entire Western Hemisphere with quarters and hope to find the one that's marked (blindfolded) to explain those odds.

Remembering that there can only be one true God, we can eliminate all the false ones by the very same processes, to see who does not fulfill these requirements.

Honestly, by any method or calculation you use to determine who God is or which god would be right for you, all of human history, all reason, all evidence, and all logic point solely to the God of the Bible.

You and I are only two lone souls among the myriads of those who have lived and died since the beginning of time. It seems that for us to make the determination of who God is, based on our own feelings would be a pretty bold move.

As you examine history, you find that many millions of people have examined the Bible for proof and, based on their findings, concluded that the God of the Bible is the real God. Many of these started out as enemies of God.

This also includes many people who lived during the time of Christ, as well as people who knew the authors that wrote what we call the New Testament. It is a safe bet that if you were living at that time and knew the ones writing, you would also know if they were writing about truth or about lies. There is overwhelming evidence that the people alive back then who examined their facts chose the God of these authors.

Although the entire New Testament as we have it was not officially accepted as scripture until 400 AD, all of the books contained in it were written before 100 AD, and universally accepted at that time by all early church Christians.

There were high standards set for a book to be accepted as Scripture and placed in the New Testament of the Bible. These included, as mentioned earlier, that the book must be written by an apostle (such as Peter, Paul or John), a close associate of an apostle (such as Mark or Luke), or a close associate of Jesus (such as James or Jude). Second, the book must accurately portray Jesus and be true to basic Christian teachings. Third, all of the first-century churches would have recognized these teachings as true and reliable, so it was also required that these books be accepted as genuine by them. And then finally, trust that God would see to it that the proper books were placed in the final draft.

Because of these standards, we can see that books that were written afterward, many hundreds of years after Christ and the apostles, such as the Qur'an or the Book of Mormon, are not and cannot be considered to be from God.

There are two points. If the Bible is truth, then nothing can (or needs to) come after it. By all standards it is the complete and finished Word of God.

And, if the Bible is not truth, then these later books that use the Bible as a source for their content cannot be truth either. Either they are a lie, or they are based on a lie, but either way, they are books of lies. If there is any truth, it can only be found in the Bible, which is the source of all truth.

Chapter Sixteen

THE CHANGE OF LIFE

I promised at the beginning that these last couple chapters would be life changing if you got to them. That change will only come, of course, if you choose the right God. This is the God that is right for you. History, evidence, and personal testimonies of others who have chosen the right God verify that this true.

Throughout your life, you have been digging a pit for yourself through the series of choices that you have made. Now, by making the right choice, you can begin to fill that pit back in and work your way back to level ground.

The Bible says that when you choose the right God, He will come into your life, save you from your sin and the death that comes as a result of that sin and help you rebuild your life. He will give you a new perspective. One that is contrary to anything that you believed to be right before. He will make you a new creation—kind of like a professional makeover, but from the inside out.

The Bible is laced with promises from God, and as a personal testimony, I believe all of them to be true and have experienced incredible intervention in my life by God as a result of my faith in Him. He will extend this help to you as well because He promises to, and He is faithful to keep His Word.

The process to make the right choice and get yourself right with the real God is not as complicated as you may think. In fact, it is quite simple. First, it is important to understand that you do not have to change yourself in order to make yourself more worthy of God's acceptance.

The truth is you can't. There's absolutely nothing you can do to make yourself right with God, or right for God. There is no amount of money you can pay that would be enough. Nor is there is any amount of good things that you can do. Hoping, wishing, or thinking that you have done enough good to outweigh your bad will not work, because outweighing bad does not make bad go away. It only helps disguise it a little bit.

The only thing that can pay enough for your sin, or make the bad go away, is the redeeming payment that Jesus made for your sin by dying on the cross at Calvary. Jesus made this payment on your behalf. God makes this benefit available to you for free by faith alone. When you trust by faith that what Jesus did on the cross was good enough to pay your debt to God for the sin in your life, God accepts your faith and sets you free from your responsibility to pay for that sin yourself. Because of your faith in Jesus, the real God takes you into His family and gives you eternal life. It's really that simple, and once you reach that point, the rebuilding and growth period begins.

The steps to your salvation (being saved by God from your sin) begin with your true inner thoughts. God knows your thoughts and, therefore, knows if you are sincere. If you truly want to have a relationship with Him, He knows that. What God seeks is an honest attitude between you and Him. He wants you to admit to Him face to face (thought to thought) that you are a

The Change Of Life

sinner. He already knows that. He wants you to know that you know that.

Once you admit to God that you're a sinner, you have to acknowledge to Him that you know that there is nothing you can do about it. Tell Him that you are now aware that Jesus paid the price for your sin, and you are sure that there is nothing else that has to be done, because Jesus did it all on the cross at Calvary. Tell Him that you trust that, and that you know, through Jesus, you are saved forever.

As you accept Jesus as your Savior, the Bible teaches that God sends His Spirit to live beside your spirit. He does this in order to help you grow in His grace and knowledge. God's Spirit will lead you and guide you as you submit your will to His.

One of the ways God uses to help you grow is through His Word, the Bible. It is extremely important that, as a follower of Christ, you find a way to read at least a little bit in your Bible every day. As hard as it is to understand at first, the Bible is living and powerful. It has the power to change lives. As you study it, your life will transform.

Trying to read the Bible without some sort of plan can be difficult. There are, however, a variety of ways available to help make this easier for you. If you've never been in the Bible before, or at least not much, then I personally suggest that you start out by reading the Gospel of John. This is the fourth book in the New Testament and is a great place to start. If you don't have a Bible, or if you like to read online, Biblegateway.com has free access to many different Bible versions and commentaries.

Another good way to start each day is with a daily Bible devotional, such as Our Daily Bread©, which has a daily Bible passage reference to look up and read, followed by a brief story application. There is one for each day of the year. Our Daily Bread© is a free publication, or is also available online at rbc.org.

Another equally handy tool for daily bible study is the Word of Life Quiet Time Diary© with commentary, which is available through Word of Life Fellowship, Inc (wol.org).

There are, of course, a number of good daily devotionals to choose from, but I caution you that not all of them are scripturally sound, so make sure that you do your homework and only acquire a daily devotional from a known-to-be-reputable organization. The ones I have mentioned here are true to God's Word and reliably accurate. It would pay to at least start with these, and then, as you become more acclimated with God's truth you can branch out from there.

> It matters not how strait the gate, how charged with punishments the scroll. I am the master of my fate: I am the captain of my soul.
> ~William Ernest Henley (1849-1902)

Another bit of advice that may help you succeed in finding time each day is to have your Bible devotions first thing in the morning. For me, I tend to unknowingly reclaim my right to be master of the universe overnight, so when I wake up in the morning, without some Word from God first, I head out trying to do everything according to my own understanding. On top of that, if I plan to do my Bible reading later, later often never comes.

If someone offered to give you the key that unlocks the riches of the world, and all you had to do was set your alarm a half-hour earlier so you could read the instructions, would you say no? If you adjust your schedule just a little, this morning time spent in the Bible will quickly become the highlight of your day.

Another way to reach a better understanding of God is through prayer. Prayer is simply carrying on a conversation with God. Again, there is certainly more than one right way or one right time to pray.

Some people use an acronym such as A.C.T.S. to help them stay focused in prayer.

A: Adoration. Tell God how great you know Him to be.

C: Confession. Even though God forgave your sin at salvation, you still sin every day and need to confess (admit) that to God.

T: Thanksgiving. Thank God for everything you can think of, because He provided it all.

S: Supplication. This means asking God for what you need and — more importantly — asking God to give others you know what they need.

Is there a right time to pray? The Apostle Paul says to pray continually. This can mean living in an attitude of prayer; talking to God throughout the day, asking for advice, thanking Him for different things and praising His intervention in your life. It would be good as well to set a specific time each day to get together with your family members and pray. Perhaps after dinner or just before bed might work best for this "official" time for prayer.

Finally, finding a local church where you can interact with other believers of like faith is crucial to Christian growth. Hebrews 10:25 says, "You should not stay away from the church meetings, as some are doing, but you should meet together and encourage each other."

There are not many churches these days that stay true to God's Word, so you will have to take some precautions when finding the right church to attend. You can't go by feelings, because feelings can mislead you, but there are indicators you can use to narrow down your search. Check first for any churches in your area that might be involved with either Word of Life Clubs (wol.org) or Awana® programs (awana.org). These are clubs that faithfully teach the Word of God to young people. A non-God-honoring church would not want to have organizations like these around. A church that ministers to its young people is a church worth attending. There are other youth and adult ministries that Bible believing churches use that are equally as effective. Make sure you investigate the doctrinal statements of both the church and the programs it uses before becoming too attached. If you go to awana.org and click on their "What We Believe" tab (under "Info for Churches"), you can read a doctrinal statement that any Bible believing church will mirror.

It would also be a good idea for now to stay away from any churches that put more emphasis on devotion to a denomination rather than Jesus. He should be at the forefront of whatever church you attend.

IN CLOSING

If this book has helped you to either choose the right God, or in some way helped you to grow closer to Him, then I encourage you to email us and let us know. Our email address is savedone95@gmail.com.

The Bible says, "Let the redeemed of the LORD say so, Whom He has redeemed from the hand of the enemy" (Psalm 107:2 [NKJV]) and, "If you declare with your mouth, 'Jesus is Lord,' and if you believe in your heart that God raised Jesus from the dead, you will be saved" (Romans 10:9).

We would like to help you do that (declare that Jesus

The Change Of Life

is your Lord) by placing your name on our website as one who has put their faith and trust in Jesus for their salvation. Our website address is whichgodshouldichoose.com. This will be your chance to proclaim across the World Wide Web that you chose the right God.

> I have no fear, though strait the gate, He cleared from punishment the scroll. Christ is the Master of my fate; Christ is the Captain of my soul.
> ~Dorothea Day (early 1900s)

FOR FURTHER STUDY

One of my favorite authors and speakers is Dr. John Barnett. He is a very interesting and knowledgeable teacher that you can trust. If you Google his name or go to dtbm.org you can find out more about him.

Ray Prichard is another personal favorite that you will also like. You can find out about him at keepbelieving.org, and also listen to sermons, watch videos, or buy his books there.

Other truthful authors that you can trust are Dr. Erwin Lutzer, Woodrow Kroll, Adrian Rogers, and Ken Ham.

I would also recommend going to wol.org and checking out their summer speaker schedule. Most of these guest speakers are also authors and can be trusted to share God's Word accurately.

Also, while there, you may want to check out the summer camping schedule. Word of Life, in Schroon Lake, New York, has week-long Bible conferences throughout the summer with campsites available at the Word of Life Family Campground, or deluxe rooms at the Word of Life Inn. The Bible teachers that speak at these week long retreats are among the finest in the world.

Finally, I encourage you to visit the Creation Museum in Petersburg, Kentucky. They do far more than counter the evolutionist's phony claims; they prove that they cannot possibly be true. You can also learn more about creation at answersingenesis.org.

NOTES

1. http://www.religioustolerance.org/dc_jones.htm
2. http://en.wikipedia.org/wiki/Branch_Davidians
3. http://en.wikipedia.org/wiki Marshall_Applewhite
4. http://en.wikipedia.org/wiki/Bonnie_Nettles
5. "Bo and Peep." *Wikipedia*. Wikimedia Foundation, 21 Dec. 2012. Web. 22 Dec.2012.
6. Balch, 2002, p. 211 West, Cornel, and George Yancy. *Cornel West: A CriticalReader*. Malden, MA: Blackwell Pub., 2001. Print.
7. http://en.wikipedia.org/wiki/Comet_Hale-Bopp
8. http://en.wikipedia.org/wiki/Heaven's_Gate_(religious_group); Balch, 2002,p. 211. West, Cornel, and George Yancy. *Cornel West: A CriticalReader*.Malden, MA: Blackwell Pub., 2001. Print.
9. http://en.wikipedia.org/wiki/Heaven's_Gate_(religious_group)#Mass_suicide_and_aftermath
10. http://wiki.answers.com/Q/How_many_gallons_of_oil_does one_supertanker_ship_carry
11. http://en.wikipedia.org/wiki/Mars
12. http://www.gotquestions.org/Jehovahs-Witnesses.html
13. http://www.gotquestions.org/Jehovahs-Witnesses.html
14. http://www.gotquestions.org/Christian-science.html

15. http://en.wikipedia.org/wiki/List_of_religious_populations; Top Ten OrganizedReligions of the World – Infoplease.com
16. http://www.bahai.com/thebahais/pg17.htm
17. http://www.bahai.com/thebahais/pg17.htm
18. http://www.bahai.com/thebahais/pg17.htm X
19. http://www.pbs.org/empires/islam/profilesmuhammed.html
20. http://www.pbs.org/empires/islam/profilesmuhammed.html
21. (Reference Islam, George Braswell Jr.)
22. Amniat. "NCTC Report on Terrorism 2011." *Scribd.* N.p., n.d. Web. 22 Dec.2012.; http://articles.nydailynews.com/2010-12-13/news/27084256_1_glenn-beck-muslims-terrorists
23. http://www.gotquestions.org/Shintoism.html
24. http://en.wikipedia.org/wiki/Asceticism#Mahavira.27s_asceticism
25. Jacobi, Hermann (1884). (ed.) F. Max Müller. ed (in English: translated fromPrakrit). The Kalpa Sutra. Sacred Books of the East vol.22, Part 1. Oxford: TheClarendon Press. ISBN 0-7007-1538-X. http://www.sacred-texts.com/jai/sbe22/sbe2200.htm, Note: ISBN refers to the UK:Routledge (2001)reprint. URL is for the scanned version of the original 1884 reprint.
26. Shouler, Kenneth. "The five vows of Jainism." http://www.netplaces.com/world-religions/jainism/the-five-vows-of-jainism.htm
27. http://urantiabook.org/archive/readers/601_jainism.htm
28. http://www.cnn.com/2012/08/06/us/sikhs-bias-crimes/index.html
29. http://www.cnn.com/2012/08/06/us/sikhs-bias-crimes/index.html
30. http://en.wikipedia.org/wiki/Guru_Nanak

Notes

31. http://en.wikipedia.org/wiki/Sa%E1%B9%83s%C4%81ra
32. http://www.gotquestions.org/buddhism.html
33. http://www.gotquestions.org/hinduism.html
34. radaronline.com, Steven Hassan.
35. http://unificationnews.com/article unification_church_faithful_gather_in_south_korea_to_mourn rev__moon
36. Mormon Doctrine, p. 321; Joseph Smith, Times and Seasons, vol. 5, p. 613-614;Orson Pratt, Journal of Discourses, vol. 2, p. 345; Brigham Young, Journal ofDiscourses, vol. 7, p. 333.
37. Mormon (Doctrines and Covenants 130:22).
38. Teachings of the Prophet Joseph Smith, p. 345.
39. Teachings of the Prophet Joseph Smith, p. 345-347, 354.
40. Articles of Faith, by James Talmage, p. 443.
41. Mormon Doctrine, p. 516.
42. gold plates Joseph Smith supposedly found
43. http://www.oprah.com/spirit/Oprah-Talks-to-Eckhart-Tolle
44. http://westerngh.com/2010/04/oprah-winfrey-opens-church-founds-religion/
45. http://www.religionfacts.com/a-z-religion-index/unitarian_universalism.htmbeliefs
46. http://www.gotquestions.org/scientology-Christian-cult.html
47. http://www.path2prayer.com/article/541/victory-overcoming-temptation/dying-to-self, Review and Herald, April 10, 1894
48. http://en.wikipedia.org/wiki/Personal_finances_of_professional_American_athletes
49. http://articles.businessinsider.com/2012-03-23/news/31228384_1_drugs-prisoners-jail
50. http://www.kuam.com/story/19483700/computers-an-afterschool-necessity-for-many-young-students

51. From the Census Bureau web page:http://www.census.gov/population/www/socdemo/hh-fam.html
52. http://www.learn-about-alcoholism.com/statistics-on-alcoholics.html ;http://www.womansavers.com/Adultery-alcoholism.asp; http://www.learn-about-alcoholism.com/statistics-on-alcoholics.html
53. http://www.fit.edu/caps/articles/facts.php
54. http://explorernews.com/news/article_80b7a2d0-c84f-11e0-971b-001cc4c03286.html
55. http://en.wikipedia.org/wiki/School_prayer
55. http://www.fit.edu/caps/articles/facts.php
56. http://www.ehow.com/info_8028762_causes-extramarital-affairs.html;http://ezinearticles.com/?Alcoholism-and-Adultery-Go-Together-Like-Bread-and-Butter&id=240360 ;
57. www.drugwarfacts.org
58. http://www.lifeevolver.com/workaholic-careful-job-killing/ (symptom and risks)
59. http://www.marriage-success-secrets.com/statistics-about-children-and-divorce.html; http://workblogging.blogspot.com/2006/03/overwork-increasingly-cited-as-reason.html (overwork - divorce trebled)
60. According to Getting Men Involved: The Newsletter of the Bay Area MaleInvolvement Network.
61. Horn, Wade F., and Andrew Bush. *Fathers, Marriage, and Welfare Reform*.Indianapolis, IN: Hudson Institute, 1997. Print.; http://www.marriage-success-secrets.com/statistics-about-children-and-divorce. html Copyright 2006-2012 Marriage-Success-Secrets.com Life Discoveries Inc. 535 Olympic DriveSlinger, WI 53086
62. http://www.mensdefense.org/STM_Book/FatherDeprivation.htm
63. (International Labor Organization 2011).

64. Press Release: "Christians Are More Likely to Experience Divorce Than AreNon-Christians." Released by the Barna Research Group, 12/21/99,www.barna.org/cgi-bin/MainTrends. asp; Barna Research Group, 12/21/99,www.barna.org/cgi-bin/MainTrends.asp; http://www.lifeevolver.com/workaholic-careful-job-killing/ (symptom and risks); Brian Willats, Breaking Up is Easy ToDo, available from Michigan Family Forum, citing Statistical Abstract of theUnited States, 1993; Arlene Saluter, Marital Status and Living Arrangements:March 1994 , U.S.. Bureau of the Census, March 1996; series P20-484, p. vi.;Wade Horn and Andrew Bush, "Fathers, Marriage, and Welfare Reform," HudsonInstitute Executive Briefing, 1997, Hudson Institute, Herman Kahn Center, 5395Emerson Way, Indianapolis, IN 46226, (317) 545-1000. Quoted and condensedfrom National Center for Policy Analysis, Policy Digest, Monday, July 28, 1997,"Making Ideas Change the World"; Andrew J. Cherlin, Marriage, Divorce,Remarriage (Cambridge, Mass.: Harvard University Press, 1981), page 71. Citedon page 77 of The Abolition of Marriage, by Maggie Gallagher; Peter Hill,"Recent Advances in Selected Aspects of Adolescent Development," Journal ofChild Psychology and Psychiatry 34, no. 1 (1993): 69-99. Cited on page 72 ofThe Abolition of Marriage, by Maggie Gallagher ; Robert F. Emery, Marriage,Divorce, and Children's Adjustment (Newbury Park, Calif.: Sage Publications,1988), pages 57 and 67. Cited on page 60 of The Abolition of Marriage, byMaggie Gallagher; Dorothy Tysse, and Margaret Crosbie-Burnett, "MoralDilemmas of Early Adolescents of Divorced and Intact Families: A Qualitativeand Quantitative Analysis," Journal

of Early Adolescence 13, no. 2 (May 1993):168-182`; Carmen Noevi Velez and Patricia Cohen, "Suicidal Behavior andIdeation in a Community Sample of Children: Maternal and Youth Reports,"Journal of the American Academy of Child and Adolescent Psychiatry 273[1988]: 349-356; Lee Robins and Darrel Regier, Psychiatric Disorders inAmerica: The Epidemiologic Catchment Area Study (New York: Free Press,1991), p. 103; Sara McLanahan and Gary Sandefur, Growing Up With a SingleParent: What Hurts, What Helps , (Cambridge: Harvard University Press, 1994),p. 41 ; Ibid, pg. 53; The Legal Beagle, July, 1984. Cited in Amneus, TheGarbage Generation, page 113; Sara McLanahan and Gary Sandefur, GrowingUp With a Single Parent: What Hurts, What Helps, (Cambridge: HarvardUniversity Press, 1994), p. 41 ; Ramsey Clark, Crime in America: Observationson Its Nature, Causes, Prevention and Control (New York: Pocket Books, 1970),p.39. Cited in Amneus, The Garbage Generation; Dewey G. Cornell, et al.,"Characteristics of Adolescents Charged With Homicide: Review of 72 Cases,"Behavioral Sciences and the Law, 5, No. 1 [1987], 11-23; epitomized in TheFamily in America: New Research, March, 1988. Cited in Amneus, The GarbageGeneration, page 216; "No-Fault Divorce: Proposed Solutions to a NationalTragedy," 1993 Journal of Legal Studies 2, 19, citing R. Knight and R. Prentky,The Developmental Antecedents and Adult Adaptations of Rapist Subtypes, 14CRIMINAL JUSTICE AND BEHAVIOR 403-426 (1987); Deborah A.Dawson, "Family Structure and Children's Health and Well-being: Data from theNational Health Interview Survey on Child Health," Journal of Marriage and theFamily, 53, pp. 573-579.

Notes

65. Shontell 2010, September 13 workaholic; "Marriages, Families, and IntimateRelationships Census Update (2nd Edition) [Paperback]." *Marriages, Families,and Intimate Relationships Census Update (2nd Edition):* Brian K. Williams,Stacey C. Sawyer, Carl M. Wahlstrom: 9780205157846: Amazon.com: Books.N.p., n.d. Web. 22 Dec. 2012.
66. http://www.gallup.com/poll/103459/questions-answers-about-americans-religion.aspx
67. Stoner, Peter Winebrenner. *Science Speaks: An Evaluation of Certain ChristianEvidences*. Chicago: Moody, 958. Print.
68. slogan created by James Jordan of the BBDO advertising agency
69. http://global.christianpost.com/news/shocking-figures-reveal-105000-christians-martyred-each-year-50976/#Mag1tILXijQkmwJm.99
70. http://en.wikipedia.org/wiki/Biogenesis
71. http://www.guardian.co.uk/science/2012/aug/16/book-written-dna-code; http://cyberbrethren.com/2011/02/19/how-much-data-can-your-dna-hold-hint-a-lot/ according to science daily; http://www.smgf.org/pages/how_it_works.jspx
72. Stoner, Peter Winebrenner. *Science Speaks: An Evaluation of Certain ChristianEvidences*. Chicago: Moody, 958. Print.

CPSIA information can be obtained at www.ICGtesting.com
Printed in the USA
BVOW011730200213

313715BV00001B/1/P